CW01468059

JUMPST/
DRAMA

Jumpstart! Drama contains more than forty engaging, practical, easy-to-do and highly motivating drama activities which will appeal to busy primary teachers who wish to enliven their practice and make more use of drama throughout their teaching.

Suitable for use across a variety of subjects and for a wide range of learning styles, the book introduces teaching practitioners to a range of drama conventions and demonstrates how to use them in the primary classroom. Organised in five clear parts, this new edition of *Jumpstart! Drama* covers the following topics:

- The relationship and link between drama and literacy
- Analysing both fiction and non-fiction texts through drama conventions
- Exploring poetry through drama conventions
- Developing role play and learning through imaginary worlds

With all activities connected to well-known texts, this fully updated second edition now reflects picturebooks and novels published in the last five years, and is ideal for busy primary teachers who wish to encourage their pupils in drama using texts in a dramatic and motivating way.

Teresa Cremin is Professor of Education at the Open University, UK, and author of numerous bestselling books, including *Learning to Teach in the Primary School* and *Storytelling in Early Childhood*.

Roger McDonald is a Senior Lecturer at the University of Greenwich, Vice President of the United Kingdom Literacy Association and author of *The Really Useful Drama Book* and *The Primary Teacher's Guide to Speaking and Listening*.

Emma Longley is a Senior Lecturer at the University of Greenwich, a primary school governor and a deputy regional leader/achievement coach for an inclusion charity.

Louise Blakemore is an experienced class teacher, curriculum subject leader and leading Literacy teacher across the South-East specialising in drama and the spoken voice.

Jumpstart!

Jumpstart! Science Outdoors
Cross-curricular games and activities for ages 5–12
Janet Barnett, Rosemary Feasey

Jumpstart! Apps
Creative learning, Games and activities for ages 7–11
Natalia Kucirkova, Jon Audain and Liz Chamberlain

Jumpstart! Wellbeing
Games and activities for ages 7–14
Steve Bowkett and Kevin Hogston

Jumpstart! Study Skills
Games and activities for active learning, ages 7–12
John Foster

Jumpstart! Philosophy in the Classroom
Games and activities for ages 7–14
Steve Bowkett

Jumpstart! RE
Games and activities for ages 7–12
Imran Mogra

Jumpstart! Creativity (2nd Edition)
Games and activities for ages 7–14
Steve Bowkett

Jumpstart! Drama (2nd Edition)
Games and activities for ages 5–11
Teresa Cremin, Roger McDonald, Emma Longley and Louise Blakemore

For a full list of titles in this series visit www.routledge.com/Jumpstart/book-series/JUMP

JUMPSTART! DRAMA

GAMES AND ACTIVITIES FOR AGES 5–11

Second Edition

Teresa Cremin, Roger McDonald, Emma Longley and Louise Blakemore

Routledge
Taylor & Francis Group

LONDON AND NEW YORK

Second edition published 2019
by Routledge
2 Park Square, Milton Park, Abingdon, Oxon, OX14 4RN

and by Routledge
711 Third Avenue, New York, NY 10017

Routledge is an imprint of the Taylor & Francis Group, an informa business

© 2019 Teresa Cremin, Roger McDonald, Emma Longley, Louise Blakemore

The right of Teresa Cremin, Roger McDonald, Emma Longley, Louise Blakemore to be identified as authors of this work has been asserted by them in accordance with sections 77 and 78 of the Copyright, Designs and Patents Act 1988.

All rights reserved. No part of this book may be reprinted or reproduced or utilised in any form or by any electronic, mechanical, or other means, now known or hereafter invented, including photocopying and recording, or in any information storage or retrieval system, without permission in writing from the publishers.

Trademark notice: Product or corporate names may be trademarks or registered trademarks, and are used only for identification and explanation without intent to infringe.

First edition published by Routledge 2009

British Library Cataloguing-in-Publication Data
A catalogue record for this book is available from the British Library

Library of Congress Cataloging-in-Publication Data
A catalog record for this book has been requested

ISBN: 978-1-138-48925-7 (hbk)
ISBN: 978-1-138-48926-4 (pbk)
ISBN: 978-1-351-03818-8 (ebk)

Typeset in Bembo
by Apex CoVantage, LLC

Contents

Contents

Acknowledgements

The authors would like to thank the children and staff of the many schools they have had the pleasure of working in as teachers and researchers. Special thanks go to the staff, students and partners of the University of Greenwich and the Open University for their support, enthusiasm and ideas. In addition they would like to thank their family and friends for the support during the writing process.

The authors recognize the risk-taking involved in teaching drama and are confident that all Primary professionals can use this book to extend their confidence and competence in using drama to teach English. Three books which the authors have referred to and which they recommend for further reading are:

Grainger, T. and Pickard, A. (2004) *Drama, Reading and Writing: Talking Our Way Forwards.* Cambridge: UKLA.

McDonald, R. (2017) *The Really Useful Drama Book: Using Picturebooks to Inspire Imaginative Learning.* Oxon: Routledge.

Richmond, J. (2015) *English, Language and Literacy 3 to 19: Drama.* Cambridge: UKLA and Owen Education.

Acknowledgements

CHAPTER 1
Drama and literacy

INTRODUCTION

Jumpstart! Drama provides a series of lively and enriching drama activities that can be used easily in the primary classroom.

There are four sections which can be dipped into. These provide rich and accessible ideas to stimulate drama in the classroom, helping teachers to:

- Use stories as a basis for drama work
- Use poetry as a stimulus for drama
- Teach non-fiction through the use of drama
- Develop role play areas and the drama opportunities they provide

THE BENEFITS OF DRAMA

There are many benefits of drama both for the children and for the teacher. Drama:

- Develops the imagination
- Creates affective and cognitive engagement
- Generates talk
- Enables a variety of voices to be heard
- Enriches writing opportunities
- Deepens understanding of texts
- Bridges the gap between genres
- Creates alternative perspectives
- Increases opportunities for storytelling

In addition to the drama activities explored, the book also provides teachers with:

- Over seventy examples of quality texts to use with children across the primary phase
- A concise explanation of each drama convention to enable the ideas to be adapted to other texts
- Ideas to take the activity further providing a spring board for the conventions to be used in other areas
- An invaluable overview of the changing nature of drama in the curriculum

What you will need for the activities

For the majority of activities all you will need is the text. The texts have been carefully chosen to reflect many class libraries. Where other materials are needed these have been clearly indicated at the start of an activity.

Adapting the ideas

Although ideas are presented and instructions are clearly set out, it is envisaged that teachers will use and adapt the various sections to suit their particular needs. You may for example wish to apply conventions to other texts, to mix and match conventions within texts or extend an idea and sustain it over a longer period of time.

THE CREATIVE NATURE OF DRAMA

Placed centrally on the drama continuum, with formal drama at one end and informal at the other, classroom drama enables the development of language, physical gestures, emotion, and empathy; fosters children's creative engagement; and enriches their imaginative development.

Characterised by a creative pedagogy classroom drama enables children to enter new worlds, develop their imagination, take risks, discover the unknown and consider possibilities.

Many of the ideas in *Jumpstart! Drama* will encourage you to develop opportunities for children, through the drama conventions, to think of alternatives to given situations. This possibility thinking, a hallmark of classroom drama, is situated at the heart of creativity (Craft, 2000) offering opportunities to find solutions to problems, try out ideas and conjure questions for investigation.

Classroom drama is both imaginatively and intellectually demanding, involving children in shaping new worlds whilst investigating issues within them (Cremin and Grainger, 2001). The recognition of drama as a powerful tool for learning has led to studies highlighting the positive influence of drama on writing, reading, the spoken voice, self-esteem and imagination.

Drama can develop imaginative thinking by:

- Opening up a wealth of possibilities
- Creating opportunities for decision making
- Enabling pictures and images to be conjured in the mind
- Drawing on previous experiences and memories
- Moulding what is known with what is unknown
- Providing curiosity and intrigue
- Empowering participants

DRAMA AND THE CURRICULUM

Teachers within their classrooms recognise and value the power and influence of drama. However the official status of drama as evidenced through the National Curriculum could suggest otherwise (Richmond, 2015).

Within the National Curriculum (2014) there is little mention of drama apart from within the aims of the subject of English and the non-statutory guidance and notes. It is depressing that within the non-statutory section, drama is only mentioned in relation to Year 2 and Years 3 and 4 (Upper Key Stage 1 and Lower Key Stage 2).

Reading comprehension

Year 2 non-statutory guidance and notes.

'*Role-play and other drama techniques can help pupils to identify with and explore characters. In these ways, they extend their understanding of*

3

what they read and have opportunities to try out the language they have listened to.'

Writing composition

Year 2 non-statutory guidance and notes.

'Drama and role-play can contribute to the quality of pupils' writing by providing opportunities for pupils to develop and order their ideas by playing roles and improvising scenes in various settings.'

Reading comprehension

Years 3 and 4 non-statutory guidance and notes.

'Pupils should be encouraged to use drama approaches to understand how to perform plays and poems to support their understanding of the meaning. These activities also provide them with an incentive to find out what expression is required, so feeding into comprehension.'

Writing composition

Years 3 and 4 non-statutory guidance and notes.

' They should have opportunities to create their own improvised, devised and scripted drama for each other and a range of audiences as well as to rehearse, refine, share and respond thoughtfully to drama and theatre performances.'

Taken on face value the scarceness of mentions of drama within the National Curriculum could lead the reader to think that it is no longer valued, especially coming after its inclusion in past National Curricula as well as its own strand within the renewed Primary Framework for English (DfES, 2006).

However the National Curriculum (2014) is only one part of the fuller and richer School Curriculum where schools can put the flesh on the bones of the National Curriculum by designing a creative, inspiring and imaginative curriculum drawing on the local knowledge and the local area to develop inquisitive and critical thinkers.

Jumpstart! Drama expertly compliments the School Curriculum by providing opportunities for children to:

- Work imaginatively
- Improvise and sustain the different roles they choose to adopt
- Offer ideas to develop the unfolding drama
- Contribute towards a problem-solving agenda

(Cremin and McDonald, 2013)

DRAMA, SPEAKING AND LISTENING

Drama provides opportunities for children to practice and develop their speaking and listening. First hand experiences give children something to talk about as they become physically and emotionally involved in a situation. They explore ideas and learn to communicate thoughts and feelings for a range of purposes and audiences.

Drama provides opportunities for children to:

- Generate ideas that can then be shared through talk in order to organise their thinking and develop a deeper understanding of a particular situation
- Speak clearly in an imaginary context in order to share ideas, thoughts and opinions
- Respond in role as someone else and explore others' perspectives and values through voicing these aloud
- Improve listening skills by becoming an active listener, attending to other people's opinions in order to recognise and appreciate different points of view and develop empathy
- Debate and explore ideas collaboratively for purposeful reasons, communicate evidence and reasons that justify their choices, make decisions and communicate a point of view
- Develop relevant and appropriate responses to other people's ideas, thoughts, opinions and actions by reflecting on what has been heard or seen
- Extend knowledge of words and phrases and develop understanding of language used in a variety of real and imaginary contexts for different reasons
- Adapt talk to suit formal and informal contexts, purposes and audiences

- Collaboratively interact with others in a variety of situations and contexts and evaluate the impact and effectiveness of their language, gesture and communication
- Develop understanding of characters, places and situations through interactive, collaborative role play experiences

DRAMA AND WRITING

Drama can be a powerful tool for enabling young writers to generate ideas, rehearse their ideas orally and shape the content of their writing. It is highly motivating and involves learners both emotionally and cognitively, providing both purpose and audience for their writing. The lived experience of the drama can become a natural writing frame, charged with the emotions and engagement of the imaginary scenario. As a consequence children's writing in role often has voice, verve and conviction. Try to align the drama techniques with the writing, e.g. inner monologue is aligned with diary writing.

Drama provides opportunities for children to:

- Develop what they want to say in a given imagined context
- Share ideas with others and listen to their ideas thus widening their possible options within a later piece of writing
- Write in imagined scenarios and with a stronger sense of the purpose and audience of their writing
- Connect emotionally to issues, which enables them to communicate their point of view with passion
- Find a position and perspective from which to write and the voice to communicate this on paper or screen
- Use the knowledge and insights developed about the characters, theme, plot or content of the drama in their writing
- Explore alternative perspectives and attitudes and thus voice increased empathy in their writing
- Reflect upon and deepen their engagement in the drama
- Adapt their writing to suit the particular purpose and audience, using the skills learnt in literacy in engaging and motivating contexts
- Develop independence and commitment as writers, motivated by the fictional world they inhabit

DRAMA AND READING

In essence drama focuses on language, interpretation and meaning so it is a potent tool for enabling children to explore and inhabit texts. Through the use of the different drama conventions, children can move imaginatively in and out of texts, living the moments and experiencing the emotions. Drama can be used across genres and text types, providing a creative way in which to develop comprehension, allowing children to access and understand texts in a meaningful way.

Drama provides opportunities for children to:

- Develop their language and extend their vocabulary
- Create visuals of what they see in the mind's eye
- Explore plot lines at differing depths
- Develop empathy for characters' situations
- Deepen understanding of character actions and reaction through vicariously living their experiences
- Enrich understanding of how narratives are built up and link together
- Make thoughtful predictions and draw deeper conclusions before, during and after reading the text
- Develop their inferential understanding and explore other higher level comprehension skills
- Apply the information they have deduced and interpret the ideas suggested in the text in action
- Explore language and develop an understanding of how it impacts on the reader
- Engage in response to text, no matter what reading level they are, and access more difficult texts that may be too complex when working independently
- Make personal connections to the text
- Explore issues and dilemmas from differing points of view

LEADING DRAMA IN THE SCHOOL

Drama can richly enhance the learning experiences of children, whether through informal opportunities in a role play area, through the use of standalone drama techniques, through the more extended use of drama techniques to build a fictional world or through drama that is more performance oriented. The latter might encompass assemblies, plays, performance poetry, dance drama and of course school plays as well as theatre trips and education companies visiting schools to perform their plays.

In a staff meeting

- Brainstorm all the drama events and practices that happen across the year
- Review these: are there ongoing opportunities for all young people?
- Focus on classroom drama: What drama techniques are known?
- How are the techniques used in literacy and/or across the curriculum?
- How are staff engaged in classroom drama, as watchers or as teacher in role?
- Focus on drama as performance: What opportunities are there?
- Focus on watching or participating in drama through plays, assemblies, theatre trips or theatre in education companies coming to school
- Focus on role play areas: how well planned and used are these?

Decide on a development focus – this might include

- Widening the range of drama strategies used
- Developing a bank of books to examine through drama
- Employing drama to develop inference and deduction
- Linking drama to writing more overtly
- Employing drama strategies across the curriculum

THE DRAMA CONVENTIONS

Throughout *Jumpstart! Drama* a range of drama conventions are introduced. An outline of the conventions is provided below.

Thought tracking
In this convention, the private thoughts of individuals are shared publicly. The teacher could touch individuals on their shoulder during a freeze frame, halt an improvisation or the whole class could take on the

persona of one individual and simultaneously speak out their thoughts and fears in a particular situation.

Ritual

In this convention the teacher and the class together work out ways of marking significant events in the narrative and create a scene or ritual which slows the drama down and provokes a sense of significance as well as reflection. Ritual is often used to conclude work or to intensify the tenor of the drama.

Group sculpture

In this convention groups are invited to make still images with their bodies. It may be to capture a moment in time, to explore the inner meaning of a text or to isolate a moment in the drama. It involves children in discussing and creatively capturing the theme of a text.

Role on the wall

A role on the wall is created by drawing an outline of a significant character on a large piece of paper and then adding information and feelings about them within the shape. As knowledge and understanding about the character develops through drama or further reading of the text, additions can be made to the role on the wall.

Role play

In this convention children are invited to adopt the role of a particular character. This may be done individually, in pairs or in larger groups. The strength of this convention is to enable pupils to 'get inside' the thoughts, feelings and actions of a character and explore the possibilities.

Teacher in role

In this convention the teacher engages fully in the drama by taking various roles. The technique is a tool through which the teacher can support, extend and challenge the children's thinking from inside the drama. It is the most powerful convention the teacher has at their disposal.

Decision alley

In this convention children examine the pros and cons of a decision. Two lines of children face each other. One child, in role, walks slowly down the alley. As the character progresses their thoughts or the sets of views for and against a course of action are voiced by the children forming the alley.

Forum theatre

This convention involves a few children improvising a situation in front of the class. The drama is then evaluated by those watching who talk about the things that have been said and done. The same situation is then reworked using the advice and comments that have been discussed.

Freeze frame

In this convention children create a tableau by forming still or 'frozen' statues. Freeze frames are used to stop the action or perhaps to show a memory, a wish or a dream. They work best when children are given a short time to think about what they will freeze frame and how they will do this, before getting into position. Children could physically move around as the character for a few seconds before freezing the action to help them get into role.

Hot seating

Hot seating involves a child (or the teacher) taking on the role of a character from a text. Other children ask them questions either in role as of one of other characters or as an observer outside the drama. The purpose of asking questions is to find out about the character's motives, attitudes and behaviour.

Improvisation

This convention provides an opportunity to explore a situation in role and can be spontaneous or planned. Planned improvisation gives children time to discuss the structure of the drama and script ideas beforehand, whereas spontaneous improvisation encourages an immediate response to others in role.

Sound collage

This convention is created when children make sounds with their voice, body percussion or instruments to evoke an atmosphere. This involves experimenting with ideas that express a feeling or convey a mood. A sound collage could be used to accompany a freeze frame or stand alone as a separate activity.

REFERENCES

Craft, A. (2000) *Creativity across the Primary Curriculum: Framing and Developing Practice.* London: Pembroke.

Cremin, M. and Grainger, T. (2001) *Resourcing Classroom Drama 8–14.* Loughborough: NATE.

Cremin, T. and McDonald, R. (2013) Drama. In R. Jones and D. Wyse (eds.), *Creativity in the Primary Curriculum* (pp. 83–97). London: Routledge.

DfE (2014) *The National Curriculum for England.* London: DfE.

DfES (2006) *The Primary Framework for Literacy and Numeracy* London: DES.

Richmond, J. (2015) *English, Language and Literacy 3 to 19: Drama.* Cambridge: UKLA and Owen Education.

CHAPTER 2

Exploring story through drama conventions

This chapter offers the reader 48 texts to *Jumpstart! Drama* through 12 drama conventions. Although specific texts have been chosen to act as a model for immediate use, it is hoped that the reader will see how the ideas can be adapted for use with a wide range of texts.

THOUGHT TRACKING

In this convention, the private thoughts of individuals are shared publicly. The teacher could touch individuals on their shoulder during a freeze frame, halt an improvisation or the whole class could take on the persona of one individual and simultaneously speak out their thoughts and fears in a particular situation.

Click Clack Moo Cows That Type

Age range: 5–7 years

Text: *Click Clack Moo Cows That Type* by Doreen Cronin (Simon and Schuster, 2003)

- Introduce the front cover. Explore what surprises the children about the picture and title of the book. When reading invite the children to join in the repeated lines.
- Read to the part where Farmer Brown is about to receive his second note. Ask children to turn to their partner and imagine what the cows may be demanding. Have some fun with the suggestions.
- Farmer Brown is annoyed with the animals. Imagine that he is stomping around the farm muttering under his breath. Invite the

children to be in role as the Farmer, to stomp around the room muttering under their breath. As any point freeze the children and invite some to voice their mutterings out loud!

- The cows and hens are on strike and Farmer Brown is furious. At this point invite children to form a circle around an imaginary typewriter. As they come up ask them to think about what Farmer Brown would be thinking and feeling.
- As the circle forms the teacher in role should lead the class by first touching the chair in the middle of the circle and speak out one of Farmer Browns thoughts ('This just can't go on! I am determined to get my farm back – whatever it takes!').
- When children are ready they touch the chair and speak the farmer's thoughts. An assistant could note down on a flip chart what the children are saying to form the basis of follow on work, for example the letter that the farmer would type back to the cows.

The Big Book of Happy Sadness

Age range: 5–7 years

Text: *The Big Book of Happy Sadness* by Colin Thompson (Random House Australia, 2008)

- Before showing the book, discuss with the class whether they have any pets. Lead the conversation onto how they came to own their pet. Ask if anyone has visited a pet rescue center.
- Share the front cover of the text and compare the illustration to the one on the title page. What do the children notice? Focus on one of the characters and ask children to describe how the character may be feeling.
- Read first double page to the children. Take time to explore the illustration and identify the significance of the empty space between the Grandmother and George.
- You may want to build up a picture of George and his feelings as you read the text by using the role on the wall convention.
- Read to the point where we are told that George and the Dog are seeing a reflection of themselves.
- In groups invite children to form a freeze frame of this moment. One child would be George, another taking the role of the dog and the rest depicting the bars separating them from each other.
- Tell the children that you are going to touch some of them on the shoulder and they should speak their thoughts and feelings. Maybe George wishes he could take the dog away from this place, maybe the dog is hoping that George has enough money to buy him!
- Praise the groups for their responses and invite them to note their ideas down on big thought bubbles to add to a display which could be built up throughout the unit of work.

Jumanji

Age range: 7–11 years

Text: *Jumanji* by Chris Van Allsburg (Anderson Press, 2012)

- Display the word 'Jumanji' and ask the children to discuss what they know about it. Due to the prominence of the film some children may be unaware that it originated as a story in 1981 by Chris Van Allsburg.
- In order to introduce the text to the children you could possibly give each group one of the illustrations to discuss. What is happening in the picture? What part of the story do they think it is? What may have happened before the picture and what might happen after the picture?
- As you read, stop at pertinent points to identify clues in the text which possibly warn of the danger in starting the game 'Jumanji!'
- There are many places to thought track the characters. You may be interested to explore the developing thoughts through the text. How, for example, does Peter react with the first experience of the lion appearing? You could ask the children to role play this moment, freezing the action at the point Peter sees the lion. Thought track his thoughts, possibly noting them on a flip chart.
- Build the disbelief in what is happening through the text as the children encounter monkeys, a monsoon, a guide, tsetse fly, rhinos, a python and a volcano. These provide multiple points to stop and thought track the characters.
- It may be interesting to imagine, after the game has been played, Peter and Judy tell their closest friends about their experience. Role play this discussion before freezing it to discover the interior monologue of their friends. Maybe one friend has total disbelief; maybe another knows or has experience of the game 'Jumanji!'

The Lion and the Unicorn

Age range: 7–11 years

Text: *The Lion and the Unicorn* by Shirley Hughes (Red Fox, 2000)

- Read the first two pages up to the point when Lenny remembers saying goodbye to his Dad.
- Lenny wishes he could speak to his father, to say those words which were in his mind but just did not come out.
- Invite the children to form a circle around a chair with an imaginary picture of his father on. When the children are ready they step forward, touch the chair and speak the thoughts and feelings of Lenny.
- Invite the class to recreate the scene at the railway. Count down from 5 to 1, at which point the children freeze. As you walk amongst them touch some children on the shoulder inviting them to speak their thoughts and feelings at that time.
- An assistant could note down the responses to form part of the follow up work. For example the journal entry made whilst on the train when the emotion of separation is still raw.

> **TAKE IT FURTHER**
>
> **Thought tracking** works well in a number of ways. Stop at any point in a story which could benefit from a deeper understanding of individual characters or where responses to sensitive issues could benefit children's understanding.

RITUAL

In this convention the teacher and the class together work out ways of marking significant events in the narrative and create a scene or ritual which slows the drama down and provokes a sense of significance as well as reflection. Ritual is often used to conclude work or to intensify the tenor of the drama.

Willy the Wizard

Age range: 5–7 years

Text: *Willy the Wizard* by Anthony Browne (Red Fox, 1996)

- Invite the children to look closely at the pictures in the story. Can they spot any surprises? How does Anthony Browne use the pictures to enhance the story?
- Explore the feelings Billy would have at the start of the story. Contrast those feelings with how he would have felt when picked for the team. How have the boots helped him? Who were they from? Will they ever have to go back?
- Read to the part where Willy is scoring goals. Invite the children to think of a word or phrase that Willy would say whilst scoring the goal. It may be something he has learnt about himself or may be something he wants to say to the mystery person.
- Children recreate the goal scoring (maybe on the playground) and call out their word or phrase. These could be collected and used back in the classroom at the end of the story. Children could write their words on a cut-out football or imagine they leave a note of thanks at the pie factory.

Grandpa

Age range: 5–7 years

Text: *Grandpa* by John Burningham (Red Fox, 2003)

- This sensitive text could be used in discussions or topics amongst other things about relationships, families, death or special people.
- Explore with the children the range of activities Grandpa does with his granddaughter. What do we know about the characters, their friendship and their love?
- You may want to invite the children to form a freeze frame of one of these times and then thought track the thoughts of Grandpa and his granddaughter.
- The last pictures shows Grandpa's empty chair and the assumption is that he has died. The girl wants to leave something on the chair for him.
- In groups give the children a range of materials. Invite the children to make something which reminds them of the time they spent with him.
- This could be an object from the story or a symbolic picture. For example they may make an ice cream or a skipping rope or possibly a vibrantly coloured picture.
- When putting the object on the chair they may want to think of some words of significance to go with it.

The Green Ship

Age range: 7–11 years

Text: *The Green Ship* by Quentin Blake (Red Fox, 2000)

- Keep the front cover of the story covered. Discuss with the children if they have ever explored somewhere with a friend. Where was it? What was it like? How did it make you feel?
- Read to the point where the children see something 'absolutely astonishing'. What could this be? Invite the children to draw what they may be looking at.
- The children in the text look at the map and imagine voyaging to new places. Explore with the children where these places could be. They could draw maps of distant lands in need of exploration.
- Choose one of the maps to take the ship to. Children create an adventure that takes place either orally or written.
- The Green Ship is visited every year but slowly it is becoming a distant memory as it starts to become overgrown. Tell the children that they will create an adventure as a reminder for others.
- Invite the children in groups to capture something of their adventure (a map, picture of Mrs Tredegar, telescope, paper ship) which they will leave at the foot of one of the trees as a reminder of the special times they had.
- Imagine the children are coming to the Green Ship for the final time and in their groups come and leave their objects together with some words of significance.

The Visions of Ichabod X

Age range: 7–11 years

Text: *The Visions of Ichabod X* by Gary Crew (Harbour Publishing House, 2015)

- Spend some time exploring texts by Gary Crew in order for children to identify with his style and the mysterious nature of many of his stories.
- Ask children to research the title of the book. Ichabod means "no glory" in Hebrew and features in the Old Testament. The name was also used by Washington Irving for Ichabod Crane, the main character in his short story *The Legend of Sleepy Hollow* (1820).
- The illustrations are simply glorious and time should be spent exploring them and discussing possible interpretations.
- Read the opening where we are introduced to the caretaker of the cemetery. You may find that a useful link here would be reference to the Hardy Tree at St Pancras Old Church in the United Kingdom. You could show children the pictures of the gravestones now embedded within the roots of the tree.
- From reading the first page ask the children why the gravestone may have intrigued the caretaker.
- We read that the caretaker does not believe in ghosts or any haunting but he wanders amongst the gravestones wondering. Read up to the point where we find out about woman who may be a gypsy. Ask the children to voice the thoughts of the caretaker. What might he be thinking as he wanders through the cemetery?
- Build up questions the class has about Ichabod. They may be curious about what visions he has, who his mother is, where he has come from, what the fear is and why he is leaving objects behind.
- Work with the children to imagine what visions of the future Ichabod had. What was it what made him worry so much? Children could think about an area in your own local community and imagine what it may be like in 10 or 20 years. What are the advantages and disadvantages of any change?

- Spend time exploring the children's thoughts and feelings about environmental change. Ask them to consider it from Ichabod's point of view by identifying his fears.
- Imagine that you are on a school trip to the cemetery to look at the gravestones and to look for the grave of Ichabod. The teacher could be in role as the caretaker and ask the children to write a note to Ichabod either aiming to alleviate his fears or to tell him how they will aim to protect the environment.
- Form the ritual around the gravestone as children individually, in pairs or in groups read out their note before laying it upon the gravestone.

TAKE IT FURTHER

Ritual works well in a number of ways. For example, the children as villagers might create a chant or simple dance to thank their gods for their beneficence, or in another drama, different villagers might write prayers and make artifacts to leave at a burial site.

GROUP SCULPTURE

In this convention groups are invited to make still images with their bodies. It may be to capture a moment in time, to explore the inner meaning of a text or to isolate a moment in the drama. It involves children in discussing and creatively capturing the theme of a text.

Oliver!

Age range: 5–7 years

Text: *Oliver!* By Birgitta Sif (Walker, 2013)

- This is a wonderful story about a boy called Oliver who felt a bit different from everyone else.
- As you explore the text and illustrations with the children discuss why Oliver may feel different from other people.
- Read to the point where it says 'Oliver felt a bit different'. Use the picture as a stimulus and discuss with the children times they have experienced a similar situation. How did it make them feel? Can we understand how Oliver feels? How could we show our friendship?
- Talk with the children about times when they enjoy being by themselves (possibly in their own imaginary worlds) and times when they enjoy and appreciate the company of others. If possible share your own experiences with the children.
- The story continues and we find that Oliver meets Olivia. They have a lot in common and build a new friendship with the end of this book becoming the beginning of their story.
- In groups ask children to explore the meaning of the book and to create a sculpture with their bodies to show their interpretation of the meaning. (Belonging, friendship, difference, uniqueness).

Oscar and Hoo

Age range: 5–7 years

Text: *Oscar and Hoo* by Theo (Harper Collins, 2002)

- Use thought bubbles to explore Oscar's inner thoughts at various points at the beginning of the story. For example as he is daydreaming and then watching his parents rush around.
- Soon Oscar is alone and lost. Invite children to speak out Oscar's thoughts, worries, hopes and anxieties at this point. What would he want to say to his parents?
- As the story continues explore the relationship between Oscar and the cloud. How do they help each other?
- The cloud tells Oscar stories of his friends, the birds and long journeys over land and sea. Ask the children to tell each other one of these stories.
- Finally Oscar is reunited with his parents. Group the children and ask them to think about the message from the story. What is the meaning? (Trust, friendship, loss, families)
- Oscar and his parents had a sculpture placed at their home to remind them of the experience they had all had. Invite children to create their sculpture with their bodies to represent the meaning of the text.

Night Golf

Age range: 7–11 years

Text: *Night Golf* by William Miller (Lee and Low, 2002)

- Before reading the text ask the children how they would feel if they were not allowed to do their favourite sport because of the colour of their skin.
- Explain some of the background to the text by reading the 'Author's Note'.
- Read to the point where his father tells him that golf is just for white men. Children take the role of James and think about their thoughts, feelings and questions at that moment. When the teacher taps their shoulder they speak out, as James, his thoughts.
- James feels like a fool when with the two white golfers. Stop at this point and explore the unfairness of the situation. Children think of words to sum up the apartheid.
- Invite children to use the words to make a poem or chant that James will say getting louder and louder until the apartheid is broken. Children will represent this using their bodies and movement as well. (This could take place at the end of the text).
- Ask children to research information about the African-American situation. This could then form part of a display using work generated from the text.

The Journey

Age range: 7–11 years

Text: *The Journey* by Francesca Sanna (Flying Eye Books, 2016)

- From the title of the book discuss with the children any journeys they have been on (this could include the spectrum of the journeys to school to journeys to other countries). From the front cover what type of journey do they predict this story will be about?
- Read the first page and explore the illustration. Identify the significance in the use of colour and focus on the encroaching sea. Ask children to predict how their lives may have changed forever.
- At the point where we are told that everything has become darker and the mother has become more and more worried you may want to pause and link the story to world events.
- The family pack their belongings together and say goodbye to everyone they know. Explore how the family might be feeling. What will they miss? What feelings would they have? What might they look forward to? Discuss why, at this point, everyone is not leaving. Possibly role play the conversation between the mother and one of her friends.
- Read to the point where the children fall asleep and the mother can let her true emotions out. You may want to freeze frame this point in the story and thought track the mother's thoughts and feelings at this time.
- Read to the end of the story. You may also want to explore the brilliant work of Armin Greder. Two of his books, *The Island* and *The Mediterranean*, would complement the theme of *The Journey*.
- After exploring the theme through the texts and through world events ask the children to imagine that a statue is being built in memory of the migrants who had not survived their journey and in celebration of those who had survived their journey and made a new life for themselves.
- Pick a location for the statue linked to either *The Journey* or *The Mediterranean*. Children, in groups should create a statue depicting the message they feel the book conveys. Examples could be hope, togetherness, unity, acceptance or tolerance. Invite children to also decide what the plaque on the statue might say.

- Invite three groups at a time to create their statues with the writing for the plague on display as the other children walk around the location looking at the stature and reading the words. Repeat for the other groups.

TAKE IT FURTHER

Group sculpture works well in a number of ways. Choose a part of a text where meaning can be made. This does not always have to be at the end. Ask children to depict what the moral/purpose of the story is and model this with their bodies.

ROLE ON THE WALL

A role on the wall is created by drawing an outline of a significant character on a large piece of paper and then adding information and feelings about them within the shape. As knowledge and understanding about the character develops through drama or further reading of the text, additions can be made to the role on the wall.

Elmer

5–7 years

Text *Elmer* by David McKee (Red Fox, 2007)

- Use illustration on the front cover to introduce Elmer and his unusual appearance. Draw an outline of Elmer on a large piece of paper (or on an interactive white board). Tell children they are going to collect words and phrases that describe Elmer in the shape that has been drawn.
- Read up to the page where Elmer leaves the other elephants. Begin to record information about Elmer on the role on the wall. How would you describe him? What does he do?
- Continue reading to the point where Elmer feels that there is something wrong. Add to the role on the wall by including how he feels, what he thinks and what he does. Talk about how Elmer has changed. Why do you think he wanted to be the same as all the other elephants?
- Finish reading story and add to the role on the wall. Include details about how Elmer is special and different from all the other elephants. What do you think the other elephants think about Elmer?

The Three Little Pigs

Age range: 5–7 years

Text: *The Three Little Pigs*

- Read the story of the *Three Little Pigs* up to the point where the wolf tries to blow down the brick house.
- Talk about the things the big bad wolf does in the story.
- Draw an outline of the big bad wolf on a large sheet of paper (or an interactive white board). Record information about the wolf on the inside of the outline.
- On the outside of the outline children could record what they, or the pigs, think about the wolf.
- Talk about the story endings that have been presented in different versions of the text, e.g. what happens to the wolf and the pigs?
- Use the information collected about the wolf on the role on the wall to talk about and suggest what should happen to him at the end. Should he say sorry to the pigs? Will he run away and never come back? What do you think might happen to the pigs in the future?

George's Marvellous Medicine

Age range: 7–11 years

Text *George's Marvelous Medicine* by Roald Dahl (Puffin, 2007)

- Before starting to read the text talk about what medicines are used for and the dangers associated with their use.
- Read chapter one which is all about Grandma. Draw an outline of Grandma on a large piece of paper (or on an interactive white board).
- On the inside of the shape write the things Grandma says and does using evidence from the text.
- On the outside of the shape record what the children think about Grandma based on what she says and how she treats George.
- Read chapter two about George's plan and discuss the reasons why George plans to make a medicine for Grandma.
- Add George's thoughts and feelings about Grandma to the outside of the character outline. Predict what might happen next.

Gentle Giant

Age range: 7–11 years

Text: *Gentle Giant* by Michael Morpurgo (Collins, 2004)

- Read to the end of the first paragraph on page two. Pause to talk in pairs in role as villagers to collect more ideas that describe what they think and how they feel about the Beastman of Ballyloch.
- Draw an outline of the Beastman on a large sheet of paper. Record words to describe what the villagers think, feel and say about the Beastman on the outside of the outline.
- Read up to the point where the Beastman has rescued the girl but thinks she is dead. Add words and phrases to describe the Beastman inside the outline to show his thoughts and feelings. Compare the Beastman's point of view with what the villagers said and how they felt about him.
- Continue reading to the end, pausing to talk about how the villagers' attitudes towards the Beastman change. Amend the role on the wall, perhaps using a different colour to represent the changes.

TAKE IT FURTHER

Role on the wall works well in a number of ways. It can be extended to develop a deeper understanding of the character by using the space outside the outline to record what others might think or feel about them. The space within the outline is then used to show the character's own personal thoughts, feelings and point of view.

ROLE PLAY

In this convention children are invited to adopt the role of a particular character. This may be done individually, in pairs or in larger groups. The strength of this convention is to enable pupils to 'get inside' the thoughts, feelings and actions of a character and explore the possibilities.

The Bear and the Piano

Age range: 5–7 years

Text: *The Bear and the piano* by David Litchfield (Frances Lincoln, 2016)

- Read to the point where the animals have gathered around the bear playing the piano in the forest. Ask them to turn to their partner and share what the animals might say about the magical melodies.
- Invite the children to take the role of one of the animals and when you tap their shoulder they speak out a thought, feeling, question or comment about the playing.
- Read to the point where the bear has been asked to go to the city but knows the other bears will miss him. In groups of three children should take the role of the bear, one of his friends and the girl from the city. Role play the discussion they might have.
- The girl will try to persuade the bear to come with her whereas his friends will want him to stay. This could lead on to a decision alley.
- During the role play the children will have been able to voice their thoughts. Invite them now to form two lines in the classroom. The intention will be for the bear to walk slowly through the alley, listening to the advice being given, before making a decision, at the end of the alley, about what he might do.
- Read to the point where the bear is sitting on the rooftop thinking about home. Imagine with the children that the bear goes to find the father and girl who brought him to the city. Role play the conversation as the bear persuades them that he must go home as he misses his friends.

Angry Arthur

Age range: 5–7 years

Text: *Angry Arthur* by Hiawyn Oram and Satoshi Kitamura (Andersen, 2008)

- Introduce Angry Arthur. Explore the picture on the front cover with the children. How is the character feeling? What might he be thinking? Why may he be angry?
- Read the text to the point where Arthur is told to go to bed by his mother and Arthur says no. Dramatise being shocked that Arthur would refuse his mother.
- In pairs children take the role of either Arthur or his mother. She needs to persuade Arthur to go to bed and he must convince her that he should be allowed to stay up – just this once!
- Generate ideas as a class, on the flip chart, before returning to the role play in fours and then larger groups if necessary.
- Ask some children if the class could 'listen in' to snippets of their conversations. This gives less confident participants ideas they can use.
- You may want to capture elements of the role play in shared writing led by the teacher incorporating a range of ideas from the children.

The Minpins

Age range: 7–11 years

Text: *The Minpins* by Roald Dahl (Puffin, 2001)

- This is a wonderful story about a boy called Billy who is desperate to explore the forest beyond his garden. This role play idea could be used as an introduction to the text.
- Study the front cover. What clues can we get about the story? Can you spot all the people in the picture? In the most recent version of the book Quentin Blake is the illustrator. It may be interesting to compare this version to previous versions.
- Ask the children if there has ever been something they really wanted to do but were not allowed. You may want to give your own example as well!
- Read the opening of the text. Billy wants to go into the forest but his mother won't allow him. In pairs children take the role of Billy and mother. Billy needs to persuade his mother that he should be able to go into the forest. His mother needs to come up with arguments against.
- Stop the class and ask the pairs to combine into groups of four. The same role play is then continued with more ideas being generated.
- Continue to the point where Billy is hearing voices. In groups of three children take up the roles of Billy, the voice of reason and the voice of temptation.
- Children role play the conversation that might take place. Billy listens and feeds back on what he would do based on what he has heard.

King of the Sky

Age range: 7–11 years

Text: *King of the Sky* by Nicola Davies and Laura Carlin (Walker, 2017)

- Explore with the children the different sounds, sights and tastes of home. What do they associate with the place where they live? What would they miss if they had to move?
- Read the opening of the text to the point where we are told 'This is not where you belong'. Discuss with the children how the boy would be feeling. Think about the possible reasons why he may not be in the place he would call home.
- There are some points within the text when we have the opportunity to find out more about the boy and Mr Evans. You may want to create a Venn diagram of the knowledge, experience and attitudes of the boy and also of Mr Evans. Children will see that although they have many differences they also have some core interests and similarities. This activity will help build up our understanding of the characters.
- Read to the point where the boy and Mr Evans are waiting for the return of the pigeons. Imagine that as they sit eating the Welsh cake Mrs Evans has made they start talking. Invite the children to role play this scene to find out a little more about the thoughts and feelings of the boy and Mr Evans.
- A similar role play could take place at the point where the boy is waiting for the return of his pigeon 'The King of the Sky'.
- There are many opportunities to compliment the role play with thought tracking. Choose moments in the text where the boy is thinking, sitting and waiting. These offer moments where we can explore his feelings and attitudes.

TAKE IT FURTHER

Role play works well in a number of ways. Many narrative texts lend themselves superbly for this convention. Look for gaps in the text where there is tension between the characters and use role play to explore their behaviour, attitudes, interactions and feelings. See also the non-fiction section where the same book is explored to highlight the potential for discussion.

TEACHER IN ROLE

In this convention the teacher engages fully in the drama by taking various roles. The technique is a tool through which the teacher can support, extend and challenge the children's thinking from inside the drama. It is the most powerful convention the teacher has at their disposal.

That Rabbit Belongs to Emily Brown

Age range: 5–7 years

Text: *That Rabbit Belongs to Emily Brown* by Cressida Cowell (Orchard, 2007)

- Read the opening pages. What does Stanley mean to Emily? Children should think of as many reasons why Emily never wants to part with Stanley.
- After the rainforest adventure invite the children to make up where Emily and Stanly may go next.
- After Emily puts the note on the garden gate teacher goes into role as the Queen who desires the rabbit.
- Confidently tell the children to come to you because you wish to talk to them about handing the rabbit over. Have fun in role trying to persuade the children to part with Stanley.
- Tell the children that your army will come and get Stanley unless you are convinced he should stay with them. You expect letters/ pictures of persuasion by midafternoon!

There's a Bear on My Chair

Age range: 5–7 years

Text: *There's a Bear on My Chair* by Ross Collins (Nosy Crow, 2016)

- Explore the front cover with the children. What do they notice? What surprises them? What puzzles them? Why is there a bear on the chair!?
- Whilst reading, build up a profile of the bear and the mouse. You may want to focus on how they are feeling. Throughout the story (apart from the last page) the bear remains content with sitting on the chair seemingly oblivious to the increasing frustrating figure of the mouse.
- You may want to read the story all the way through with the children before returning to it and taking on the role of the bear yourself!
- Re-read the story stopping at a suitable point where you adopt the role of the bear on the chair. Maybe act in a nonchalant way, pleased to be sitting on what you believe is your chair.
- The children should form groups of four in order to come up with a reason why you should leave the chair. Give children time to practice how they will try to persuade you to leave the chair. The children could also practice the actions they might use.
- Invite the groups to try to persuade you. As they present their ideas respond in a suitable way in line with the character of the bear in the text.
- Once all the groups have presented you could vacate the chair and offer the opportunity for a child (or group of children) to take on the role of the bear.

The Giant's Necklace

Age range: 7–11 years

Text: *The Giant's Necklace* by Michael Morpurgo (Walker Books, 2017)

- This is an emotional story which has a 'penny drop' moment for not only us as readers, but also for Cherry. The power of this story is that the moment of realization may be simultaneous for the reader and for Cherry.
- Explore Cherry's thoughts and feelings as she realises that the sea is gradually encroaching on her. The language Morpurgo uses here is rich in description.
- Encourage the children to take the role of Cherry as she scrambles up the cliff face. Use techniques such as thought tracking and decision alley to build a picture of her situation.
- With children still in role as Cherry, narrate the part of the story where she sees two men in the corner of the cave. Pick a suitable object to hold to show that you are also going into role as one of the miners.
- Beckon the children to gather round you as you tell the tale of the winding caves. Once you have created the picture in their minds ask some of the children questions to explore Cherry's situation.
- Tell Cherry that if she really wants to find her way home you will help her.
- In groups have children draw and write the description of the meeting and the walk through the winding cave to the sunlight and hopefully home.

Jemmy Button

Age range: 7–11 years

Text: *Jemmy Button* by Jennifer Uman and Valerio Vidali (Templar, 2012)

- This book is inspired by the true story of Jemmy Button who was brought to England from Tierra del Fuego in order to be 'civilized'. It would work well with the book *Wild* by Emily Hughes.
- It may be pertinent to investigate the journey of HMS Beagle with the children by way of an introduction to the text.
- Read to the point where the men are 'inviting' the boy to come away with them. Thought track the boy at this point to discover what he imagines, what he hopes and also his anxieties.
- Whist on the long voyage to England narrate the fact that Jemmy went to sleep and dreamt about what he might encounter the next day. Working from what we are told on the first page that Jemmy imagined what it would be like on the other side of the ocean, invite children to form freeze frames of one of one image from one of his dreams.
- As you read create a Venn diagram of the similarities and differences between Jemmy's home and England.
- Read to the point where we are told that sometimes he missed the island. Take on the role of Jemmy Button explaining that you are confused. Although you wanted to find out about this place you also miss home. Explain some of the things you enjoy but also that, in your heart, you know you are not settled.
- The rest of the class could be in role as the people from the town where Jemmy is. They have seen him grow up and adapt since he arrived. Tell the children that you are going to walk through the town stopping some of the people you know to ask for their advice.
- Set the town scene up in the classroom. Narrate your way into the scene and walk through the town stopping the children in role to ask for help, advice or reassurance.
- Return to your original position and reflect on what you have been told. Decide that you do hope to return home.

- On the voyage home you could repeat the dream freeze frame. Maybe children will image that he dreams that his home will be the same, maybe others will predict changes which may have taken place.

TAKE IT FURTHER

Teacher in role works well in a number of ways. This is a powerful convention in which you can change the drama from the inside and respond instantly to children's suggestions. The teacher could take practically any role from a text and explore the potential.

DECISION ALLEY

In this convention children examine the pros and cons of a decision. Two lines of children face each other. One child, in role, walks slowly down the alley. As the character progresses their thoughts or the sets of views for and against a course of action are voiced by the children forming the alley.

The Lion Inside

Age range: 5–7 years

Text: *The Lion Inside* by Rachel Bright and Jim Field (Orchard books, 2016)

- The illustrations in the text are absolutely wonderful. Before you start you may want to show the children pictures of the mouse from different points in the story. Ask the children to talk about how the mouse is feeling. Maybe you could ask the children to show a range of feelings through their expressions.
- Tell the children the story you are about to read is also about being afraid of something. Ask the children whether there is anything they are afraid of. How have they overcome their fears?
- As you read the story ask the children to make comparisons between the mouse and the lion. How are their characters different? How do other characters in the story perceive them? Maybe ask the children to move around the classroom. When you call out 'Lion' they should move how they imagine the lion in the story would move. When you call out 'Mouse' they should move as they imagine the mouse would move.
- Read to the point where the mouse needs to decide whether to ask the lion to teach him to roar. On this double page there are a range of illustrations to note with the children; the mouse reading his 'how to roar' book, the lion sitting with the mouse on his plate for dinner and the mouse gazing through the window up to the rock where the lion sleeps.
- Narrate the thought process of the mouse focusing on how confused he is and how he really does not know what to do.
- Invite the children to get into pairs and decide what advice they would give the mouse. Give time for the children to practice

their piece of advice focusing on their tone, facial expressions and gestures.

- Ask the children to form the decision alley and then choose a child (or adult) to be the mouse. The mouse should walk slowly through the alley listening to the advice being given before deciding, at the end of the alley, what decision they will make.

Pirates Love Underpants

Age range: 5–7 years

Text: *Pirates Love Underpants* by Claire Freedman and Ben Cort (Simon and Schuster, 2012)

- This humorous text would work will together with *The Pirates Next Door* by Jonny Duddle and *The Night Pirates* paperback by Peter Harris.
- Start by asking the children what they associate with pirates. If possible use props to create intrigue and curiosity. There are many ways in which children can find their own pirate name! If appropriate explore this with the children and ask them to introduce themselves to the rest of the class or group in true pirate fashion!
- Read the story and explore the pictures up to the point where we are told that the Captain has a cunning plan.
- Arrange the children into groups and invite them, in role as the pirates, to come up with their cunning plan. Give time for each group to think of the best plan they can before needing to present it to the rest of the crew.
- Once each group has decided on their plan they should present it to the rest of the class (crew) in role as the pirates.
- The teacher will act as the Captain and decide on the best plan.
- Once you have decided which you think is the best plan (still in role as the Captain) voice the doubts you also have about the plan. It's the best plan you have but you are undecided. Ask the children (in role as the pirates) to help you decide what to do.
- Children should form two lines waiting for you, in role as the Captain, to walk down the alley offering advice for what you should do.
- Once you have heard the advice, still in role as the captain, gather your crew around you and set out the details of the plan.

The Birdman

Age range: 7–11 years

Text: *The Birdman* by Melvin Burgess (Andersen, 2000)

- Share the illustration on the first page depicting the market scene.
- Consider the range of activities which might take place in the market such as selling, performing and socialising. Create the opening scene with the children by inviting them to take on the role of one of the market traders.
- When the birdman comes in calling 'birds for sale' signal the children to suddenly stop and stare.
- In this moment frozen in time, thought track some of the market traders to find out what they are thinking regarding the Birdman.
- Ask the children to explore why the robin wept. How was it feeling? What kind of life had it had? How did it become to be in a cage? What do they think about caged animals?
- His mother tells Jarvis that it is cruel to keep the bird in the cage and in Jarvis's heart he knows she is right however Jarvis kept the cage door closed.
- Narrate to the children the predicament Jarvis is in. Outline some of the tensions he would be feeling and invite the children to form two lines to explore what decision Jarvis should take.
- One child, in role as Jarvis, walks down the alley listening to the views. Once all views have been heard Jarvis should tell the group what he would do.
- The picture showing the result of his decision is powerful. Enlarge the page if possible or give groups a copy each and ask them to label it with their initial thoughts.

Black Dog

Age range: 7–11 years

Text: *Black Dog* by Levi Pinfold (Templar, 2012)

- Show the first full-page illustration of Mr Hope in the kitchen. Invite the children to examine the illustration and consider what they know is happening, what they think could be happening and what questions they have.
- Focus on the exaggeration taking place. We are told that the Black Dog is: as big as a tiger, the size of an elephant, as big as a Tyrannosaurus rex and then the size of a Big Jeffy! You could ask children to imagine what a Big Jeffy could be or to think of what the next two comparisons could be in the sequence.
- Read to the point where Small Hope is deciding whether to go outside or not. The family does not want Small to go outside to confront the Black Dog.
- Invite the children to decide whether they think Small should go. Should the youngest (and smallest) member of the family really go and face the Black Dog? Children should form two lines in the classroom for Small to walk through hearing their conscience.
- Once Small has heard the opinions ask them whether they would go and face the Black Dog and why.
- The double page illustration of Small and the Black Dog is glorious. Spend time examining the illustration (note the rabbits playing in the bottom left hand section of the page).
- Ask the children to imagine what the facial expression of Small would be. In the double page we cannot see it. You may want children to think of two facial expressions. Firstly the one Small would make when first seeing the dog and then the one as the conversation started.

> ### TAKE IT FURTHER
>
> **Decision alley** works well in a number of ways. Find any point in a story where a character faces a predicament and the choice will determine the following part of the story. Children explore the inner conflicting thoughts of the character at that point.

FORUM THEATRE

This convention involves a few children improvising a situation in front of the class. The drama is then evaluated by those watching who talk about the things that have been said and done. The same situation is then reworked using the advice and comments that have been discussed.

I Want a Pet

5–7 years

Text: *I Want a Pet* by Lauren Child (Frances Lincoln, 2000)

- Talk about the pets children have at home or are familiar with. Give time for children to share their stories about their own pets.
- Move the conversation on to consider what animals might not make such good pets. You may want to give some of your own examples and reasons why they would not make a good pet.
- Read up to the page where the child talks to her mum about having a bat. Recall the reasons why she can't have a lion, a sheep, a wolf, an octopus, a snake or a bat.
- In pairs invite the children to choose an animal. Ask them to think of a reason why they might like to have their chosen animal as a pet and a reason a parent or family member might give for not having one.
- Model the role play discussion between the child and the parent. Give time for the children to practise what the characters say to each other in role as the child and the adult.
- One pair should share their conversation in front of the rest of the class. The rest of the class could discuss what they think and make suggestions to develop the scene, e.g. What could the child say that would be more persuasive? What other ideas can you think of to agree or disagree?
- The same pair could then dramatise the same situation using ideas collected during the class discussion.

Misery Moo

Age range: 5–7 years

Text: *Misery Moo* by Jeanne Willis (Andersen, 2006)

- Talk with the children about times when they have felt miserable about friendships. What happened? What did someone say or do to cheer up?
- Explore the front cover of the text with the children. Discuss how the cow might be feeling and ask the children to give reasons for their answers.
- As you read the text talk to the children about what they do to cheer their friends up. You could discuss how the lamb would be feeling when his attempts seem not to work.
- Read up to the page where the cow finds the lamb sitting in the puddle feeling unhappy.
- In pairs think of things the cow might say or do to cheer the lamb up. What do you think this might make the lamb say or do? Improvise the situation in pairs in role as the cow and the lamb.
- One pair could share their improvisation with the rest of the class. The children watching, led by the teacher, discuss what happened and why the characters they've seen in the drama say or do particular things. What worked well? Make suggestions to improve the way in which the characters interact, e.g. What could cow say or do to make lamb smile? How could cow convince lamb to be friends again?
- The same pair of children rework the same situation using the ideas which have been discussed as a class.

The Wolves in the Walls

Age range: 7–11 years

Text: *The Wolves in the Walls* by Neil Gaiman (Bloomsbury, 2005)

- Read up to the point where the wolves come out of the walls and the family leaves the house. First in pairs, and then in groups of four, talk about what might happen next. Think about the things each member of the family might say and do. Children take on roles of the parents and children in their group of four and practice improvising the scenario.
- One group shares their improvisation with the rest of the class watching. Children talk about the drama and suggest ideas or alternatives to develop the scene, e.g. How will the way the parents behave differ to the way the children react? How could they show the feelings of the family more effectively through what they say or how they behave? What solutions can we suggest? Have the same group of children rework the situation using ideas that have been introduced.
- Continue reading to the point where the family prepares to come out of the walls. Improvise in fours what might happen when the wolves come face to face with the family. What will they do? If wolves could talk, what might they say?
- One group then improvises their version of the scenario for the rest of the class. Children watching talk about how successfully the improvisation shows how (a) the wolves and (b) the family react in this situation. How could we develop the drama to show how the characters feel, e.g. brave, scared, angry, anxious, fearless etc.? The same group of children then reworks the drama using ideas raised in discussion.

Why the Whales Came

Age range: 7–11 years

Text: *Why the Whales Came* by Michael Morpurgo (Egmont, 2007)

- Read up to the point in chapter four where Gracie and Daniel meet the Birdman. In groups of three, talk about how the children and the Birdman might react. Improvise what they might say and do, exploring how they might feel through the way they talk, their behaviour and body language.
- One group shares their improvisation with the rest of the class. Talk about the drama from the point of view of the children and also of the Birdman. What evidence can we use from the text to justify our ideas and opinions? How successfully does the drama help us understand how they all feel?
- Prompt the children watching to suggest ideas that help us to understand more about the characters. e.g. Do the children believe the rumours about the Birdman? Will the Birdman prove them right or wrong? What else is there to discover?
- The same group of children rework the drama to take into account the ideas and suggestions provided.

TAKE IT FURTHER

Forum theatre works well in a number of ways. It is particularly useful for prompting deeper exploration of difficult situations or interactions between characters. The convention can be developed by giving the children watching, or the actors, opportunities to stop the drama and suggest changes or present and justify alternatives.

FREEZE FRAME

In this convention children create a tableau by forming still or 'frozen' statues. Freeze frames are used to stop the action or perhaps to show a memory, a wish or a dream. These work best when children are given a short time to think about what they will freeze frame and how they will do this, before getting into position. Children could physically move around as the character for a few seconds before freezing the action to help them get into role.

Suddenly!

Age range: 5–7 years

Text: *Suddenly!* by Colin McNaughton (Picture Lions, 2007)

- Use the front cover to predict what the story might be about. Talk about the story of the three little pigs and the big bad wolf. What might the wolf be trying to do in this story?
- Read the story, stopping at the page where Preston goes to the park. What do you think will happen next? Freeze frame the action in pairs, one child as the wolf and the other as Preston. Count down from 5 to 1 and ask children to freeze when they hear the word "suddenly . . . .".
- Continue reading to the page where Preston gets home and talks to his mum. Stop to talk about the picture where his mum is doing the washing up with her back to Preston, and predict what might happen next. Again in pairs, one child as Preston and the other as his mum, freeze frame what could happen "suddenly . . . ".

The Scarecrows' Wedding

Age range: 5–7 years

Text: *The Scarecrows' Wedding* by Julia Donaldson (Alison Green Books, 2014)

- Introduce the children to Betty O'Barley and Harry O'Hay. Maybe talk about the purpose of Scarecrows. Show the children pictures of some and ask if they have ever seen a Scarecrow.
- Betty and Harry decide to get married and make a list of items they may need. Ask the children what might be on their list. Compare the list the children come up with to the list in the book.
- At the point where Betty and Harry ask the cows for help invite the children to form a freeze frame of the moment and then use the thought tracking convention to find out what the characters are thinking.
- Read on to the point where Harry stops to rest and falls asleep. Tell the children that he has two dreams. The first is full of joy and excitement for his forthcoming wedding but the second depicts something which could go wrong! Invite the children to pick which dream they would like to represent through a freeze frame.
- Use the thought tracking convention to discover more about the dreams.

The Hidden Forest

Age range: 7–11 years

Text: *The Hidden Forest* by Jeannie Baker (Walker, 2005)

- Use the front cover to talk about the story setting. What is this place like? What do you think the diver might find there?
- Read the first three pages up to the point where Ben falls into the water and then gets back into his boat. Children individually create freeze frames as Ben either in the water or back in the boat. How might he be feeling? Gently touch some children on the shoulder and ask them to share their thoughts and feelings.
- Continue reading up to the page where Sophie and Ben look for sea dragons. In pairs, one as each character, talk about and then freeze frame finding something under the water, i.e. a beautifully coloured creature, a golden ring, a dark cave, a mermaid etc. You may choose to stop reading the story at this point and continue using improvisation to develop ideas that could then be used by children to write their own stories.
- On the next page where Ben senses a presence in the water, children could freeze frame what they think it could be. What is Ben going to do next? Is he too scared to move or interested to look behind him? At this point children could also make a noise to describe the tension.
- Children could draw a detailed picture of the unseen creature or character and add words that describe what it looks like and how it moves.

Memorial

Age range: 7–11 years

Text: *Memorial* by Gary Crew (Lothain, 2003)

- Gary Crew is a fabulous author whose texts often bring intrigue, curiosity and emotion. Memorial would be a poignant book to use alongside Remembrance services or topics concerning the First World War.
- Take time to explore the illustrations with the children. You may want to introduce them to the work of Shaun Tan who is not only a brilliant author but also a delightful illustrator.
- Read the first page and show the picture of the tree. Discuss with the children what we can deduce about the time frame and character relationships.
- Read to the point where Old Pa tells us that Betty planted the tree and that it is something he will never forget. Show the next double page and narrate that Old Pa started to reminisce and remember some of the experiences from the war. Some experiences brought a fond smile, others brought a tear. Looking into his eyes you could see the images so vivid in his mind.
- Invite the children to form freeze frames depicting some of the images. In the discussions leading up to the freeze frames ask the children to identify what the personal link is between their depiction and Old Pa.
- Narrate this part of the story as Old Pa remembers. As children produce their freeze frames you may want to also use the thought tracking convention to find out what some of the characters within the freeze frames may be thinking.

TAKE IT FURTHER

Freeze frames work well in a number of ways. The still image can be brought to life with a caption or/sound effects or through touching a child gently on their shoulder to share their inner thoughts whilst in role. Stop at any point in a story to explore feelings, events or a theme such as anger or jealousy to explore children's understanding of what a character might do in a story, or how they might feel in a particular situation.

HOT SEATING

Hot seating involves a child (or the teacher) taking on the role of a character from a text. Other children ask them questions either in role as one of other characters or as an observer outside the drama. The purpose of asking questions is to find out about the character's motives, attitudes and behaviour.

George and the Dragon

Age range: 5–7 years:

Text: *George and the Dragon* by Chris Wormell (Red Fox, 2003)

- Talk with the children about what they have heard about dragons. Draw connections with other texts that have dragons in them. What kind of things do they do?
- Encourage children to take on the role of a dragon, showing its characteristics through the way they move around the classroom.
- Read up to the point where it is revealed that the dragon has a secret. Talk about the fierce and terrible things he does. Imagine reasons why he might behave like this.
- In pairs or small groups plan some questions to ask the dragon to find out why he is so fierce and get more information about his secret fear of mice.
- Sit two or three children on the hot seat in role as the dragon. Inviting more than one child to sit on the hot seat in role as the same character will help to build confidence and develop a wider range of responses to other children's questions.
- The rest of the class takes turn to ask the dragon questions to find out why they like to fight and frighten people.

The Highway Rat

Age range: 5–7 years

Text: *The Highway Rat* by Julia Donaldson (Alison Green books, 2016)

- Share information and pictures about Highwaymen from the past. Talk about what they did. Introduce any unfamiliar vocabulary, i.e. highway, thief, traveler.
- Read up to the point where the Highway Rat meets the duck on his journey. Talk in pairs about what we (and other characters in the book) think about the rat. How do you think the animals feel when he stops them? How do you think they feel after he has gone? Talk about different scenarios in the book using the illustrations to support discussions about feelings and experiences.
- Hot seat different characters in the story to explore and extend their ideas and experiences. Ask characters to talk about what happened to them when they met the rat.
- Talk about the Highway Rat to explore his intentions and ideas. Why do you think he steals food? Where do you think he is going? Do you think he has always been a baddie and a beast? Plan questions we would like to ask the Highway Rat.
- Hot seat the rat to find out more about him.
- Read to the end of the story and hot seat the rat again. Ask questions to see if and why he has changed his ways.

The Tunnel

Age range: 7–11 years

Text: *The Tunnel* by Anthony Browne (Walker, 2008)

- Use the pictures and text in the story to talk about the differences between the boy and his sister. Stop at the point where the boy goes into the tunnel.
- In pairs plan questions to ask the boy and girl about themselves and how they feel about each other.
- Hot seat one child as the boy and another as his sister. The rest of the class asks questions to explore their relationship.
- Continue reading up to the point where Rose hugs her brother's statue and he returns to life. Talk with the children about what they think might have happened to the boy before he turned to stone. Talk about what they might have seen, heard and felt.
- In pairs or small groups plan some open questions to ask the boy and the girl to find out what happened and how it made them both feel. Think about changes that this might bring about, e.g. How has this experience changed the boy's behaviour? How might he now feel about his sister? How do you think she now feels?
- Sit one child on the hot seat in role as the boy and one child in role as his sister. The rest of the class asks questions. What has changed since the first time they were hot seated?

Street Child

Age range: 7–11 years

Text: *Street Child* by Berlie Doherty (Harper Collins, 2009)

- Introduce the text by talking about life in London in the 1860s, perhaps supported by visual imagery/film.
- You may like to use the painting *The Crossing Sweeper* by William Powell Frith to introduce the text.
- Gather together some artifacts which could represent the Victorian era and especially ones Jim Jarvis may have encountered.
- Read to the point where Barnie wants to know what Jim's story is. Encourage the children to discuss what they think Jim's story might be. They could base their assumptions on the painting and artifacts you have shown them.
- Using the 'role on the wall' convention start to build up a picture of Jim Jarvis.
- Read up to the end of chapter 5. Talk about the conditions in the work house, what Jim had to do there and how it felt.
- In pairs or small groups children plan open questions to ask Jim about his day-to-day life in the workhouse and why he wishes to escape.
- One child sits on the hot seat to answer questions, developing answers based on the text. Encouraging children to use their imagination to extend responses can help to develop a deeper understanding of the character which can be used to support further reading of the text.

TAKE IT FURTHER

Hot seating works well in a number of ways. It is particularly useful when children have had the opportunity to explore a character's feelings and actions through other drama conventions first, e.g. freeze frames or thought tracking. These experiences can help them to talk about ideas in greater detail and depth.

IMPROVISATION

This convention provides an opportunity to explore a situation in role and can be spontaneous or planned. Planned improvisation gives children time to discuss the structure of the drama and script ideas beforehand, whereas spontaneous improvisation encourages an immediate response to others in role.

Little Lumpty

Age range: 5–7 years

Text: *Little Lumpty* by Miko Imai (Walker, 1994)

- Sing Humpty Dumpty. Talk about what happens in the rhyme.
- Use the front cover of the text to introduce the character Little Lumpty and make links with the rhyme.
- Read up to the page where Little Lumpty is stuck on the wall and everyone comes out of their houses to see what is wrong.
- Teacher in role as the town mayor leads a spontaneous improvisation with the children in role as the townspeople. Talk together about different ways to help Little Lumpty get down and improvise different ideas in role as a class. Which will be the most successful?
- Improvisation could continue by exploring what happens when he gets down. What might Little Lumpty or his mum say? What do you think the townspeople will do?

The Enormous Crocodile

Age range: 5–7 years:

Text: *The Enormous Crocodile* by Roald Dahl (Puffin, 2001)

- Look at the front cover and read the blurb on the back of the book. Discuss what children think might happen in the story. Talk about what they know about crocodiles.
- Read up to the page where the crocodile is alone in the playground. Talk about how the crocodile has behaved, how the other animals and children have responded and why. What is the problem? How do you think it might be resolved?
- As a class with the teacher in a leading role and children in role as the animals, spontaneously improvise a meeting to discuss and decide on a plan that will teach the crocodile a lesson. What will the animals do? What will happen to the crocodile?
- Improvise what might happen next as a class based on the discussion during the meeting. Each child can take on a role as one of the animals with the teacher leading in role, perhaps as the elephant.
- Read to the end of the text and compare children's ideas with the resolution given in the story.

The BFG

Age range: 7–11 years

Text: *The BFG* by Roald Dahl (Puffin, 2007)

- Read up to the end of chapter two. What have we found out about Sophie from the text so far? What do we know about the Giant? What evidence in the text supports these views?
- Continue reading to the end of chapter four where Sophie is with the BFG in the cave. Talk about what has happened. Why do you think the BFG has taken her back to his cave? How do you think Sophie might be feeling?
- In pairs plan an improvisation to describe what might happen next. What will they say? How will they behave towards each other, e.g. body language, tone of voice? What do you think Sophie might do? Will Sophie discover that he is in fact friendly? What might the giant say or do? Will more giants appear . . . ? This plan could be captured as images in a storyboard or even in an informal script to record what is said.
- Rehearse the scene in pairs.
- Improvise the situation as planned in pairs in front of the other children. As a class compare what each group does with what we know about Sophie and the Giant from the text.

Kensuke's Kingdom

Age range: 7–11 years

Text: *Kensuke's Kingdom* by Michael Morpurgo (Egmont, 2005)

- Read the blurb and discuss the images this conjures up in our minds. Who might be with Michael when he gets washed up on the island?
- Read up to page 48 where Michael wakes up on the beach. Talk about the events that have led up to this point. How has he ended up here?
- Individually, spontaneously improvise his initial exploration of the island. What will he need to do to survive? What might he find? Who might be there already?
- Read on to page 69 where Michael meets Kensuke. What might he say? What might he do? Is Kensuke alone? In pairs spontaneously improvise what they say to each other and what might happen next.

TAKE IT FURTHER

Improvisation works well in a number of ways. Improvisations that involve use of teacher in role provide opportunities to introduce and explore issues that may help to broaden and deepen children's understanding. Finding a gap in the story where a character's motives or actions have not been fully explored or pausing at the point of a dilemma can provide rich opportunities to explore the text in more depth, through meaningful and personal experiences.

SOUND COLLAGE

This convention is created when children make sounds with their voice, body percussion or instruments to evoke an atmosphere. This involves experimenting with ideas that express a feeling or convey a mood. A sound collage could be used to accompany a freeze frame or stand alone as a separate activity.

Angry Arthur

Age range: 5–7 years

Text: *Angry Arthur* by Hiawyn Oram (Red Fox, 2008)

- The ideas here could be used in conjunction with those in the role play section that refer to *Angry Arthur*.
- Use the illustration and title on the front cover and ask 'What makes you angry? How does it make you feel?'
- Read the first three pages up to the point where his anger is compared to a thunderstorm, a hurricane and a typhoon. Select and talk about instruments, body percussion or vocal sounds that could be used to make these 'angry' sounds. Individually make and explore sounds that might be heard during extreme weather conditions.
- Take it in turns to make the sounds. Talk about how to make angry sounds by thinking about the way in which the sound is made, e.g. loud sounds made by hitting instruments hard, no rhythm, random notes etc.
- Sounds could be played simultaneously, perhaps starting off quietly and getting louder and louder as Arthur gets angrier and angrier, and then quieter as he begins to calm down. Children follow teacher's directions (perhaps using hand movements) to know when to change the sound.

The Lonely Whale

Age range: 5–7 years

Text: *The Lonely Whale* by David Bennett (Kingfisher, 1991)

- Read up to page 7 when the crew of the ship is washed up on the deserted island and they make camp. As a class freeze frame the things the sailors do, e.g. chopping wood, collecting fresh water, picking fruit. Children could create a simple sound effect to add to their freeze frame to share when the teacher gently touches their shoulder.
- Before reading on to the paragraph that describes the night of the storm, imagine what it would be like to be sailors in the camp on their first night in a strange place. What sounds can be heard? What kinds of animals or birds might live there? What sounds do the trees and the sea make? Each child can individually make sounds using body percussion or voices simultaneously.
- Talk about the mood that is being created. Are they feeling scared and frightened, or excited about their adventure?
- Organise the children into small groups. Each group chooses a sound effect that creates the atmosphere using a different instrument. Practise and then share as a round, building up tension as each group is invited to join in one at a time and then gradually stopping each group as the dawn breaks.

The Minpins

Age range: 7–11 years

Text: *The Minpins* by Roald Dahl (Puffin, 2001)

- You may want to integrate the ideas here with those presented in the role play section.
- Read up to page 12 where Little Billy is being chased by the Spitler. Break down the story so far into different parts as a class and talk about the mood at each point, e.g. entering the forest nervously, the stillness and peace of the forest, frantically being chased by the monster.
- As a class practise making sounds to represent different moods or feelings. Talk about how the sounds help to create a particular atmosphere. What happens when we use more than one sound at a time? How can a sound be changed to alter the mood? How can one instrument be used to create different sounds?
- Split the children into smaller groups. Allocate each group part of Billy's adventure. Use instruments, body percussion or voices to create a sound collage to describe the atmosphere, e.g. one group could simply chant the rhyme "beware, beware the forest of sin . . . " perhaps as a whisper, to capture an apprehensive, sinister mood.
- Perform the sound collage as a class, introducing each group at different points with the teacher or a child's direction. Groups could either play individually or simultaneously, starting and stopping at different times. The sound collage could be recorded and replayed to evaluate the success at creating an atmosphere, mood or feeling.

Skellig

Age range: 7–11 years

Text: *Skellig* by David Almond (Hodder, 2007)

- Read chapters 1 and 2 and talk about the clues that tell us about the creature in Michael's garage. What do you think it might be? How did it get there? Where has it come from?
- Talk about the atmosphere and mood at the point on page 4 where Michael stands at the garage door. What sounds can he hear? How do you think he might be feeling; scared, intrigued, nervous, excited?
- Practise individually making sounds that he might hear in the garage simultaneously as a class. Then split into smaller groups to share ideas. As a group, make a symbol to represent each sound on squares of card and put them into a sequence. Each group performs their sound collage to the rest of the class.
- As they listen, other children can think about the mood or atmosphere that is created. Share ideas, e.g. how successfully did the collage evoke a particular mood or feeling?

> **TAKE IT FURTHER**
>
> **Sound collage** works well in a number of ways. A piece of music or sequence of sounds could be created that tell a story. This may involve changing the mood or atmosphere at various points to describe different characters, events or perhaps represent a theme in the story. Children could explore the way in which sounds can be used to build up to a dilemma and then change to symbolise the resolution.

CHAPTER 3
Exploring poetry through drama conventions

This chapter offers 10 ideas to *Jumpstart! Drama* through the exploration of poetry. Using drama conventions in poetry is very similar to that of story. You need to look for poems with strong themes and enough content to provide the children with areas to explore. Drama conventions can be used before, during and after reading the poem, supporting prediction, sequencing and engagement with character. It is important to choose the moments for drama carefully, applying the conventions that best suit the purpose of the work you want the children to do. This is slightly more difficult with poetry because poems are generally shorter and the children may need more talking though into the techniques.

DRAMA AND POETRY FOR KEY STAGE 1

The Tale of the Custard Dragon

Age range: 5–7 years

What you will need: A copy of *The Tale of the Custard Dragon* by Ogden Nash (Little Brown Books for Young Children, 1998).

- Ask children to discuss with a partner what they know about dragons. How might we describe a dragon (e.g. fierce, dangerous)? So what do they think a Custard Dragon is? Why might this dragon be called Custard?
- Read verse one and two of the poem to the children. Discuss; who is the main character? Why did she call the dragon Custard?

- Read to the end of verse six. Move the children into groups and get them to share out the characters in the poem (if you need to, have two children playing Custard). Talk them into a role play showing how the group was acting towards Custard, calling him names and laughing at him. Move in between the groups adding ideas where needed to the role play. Pull all of the children playing Custard together and get them to thought track how he is feeling and why at this point in the poem.

- Read the poem verses seven to nine. How have the characters reacted to the intruder? Move children into groups to freeze frame what they think will happen next in the poem. Ask them to title their freeze frame using a phrase that explains what is happening.

- Read to the end of verse eleven. Did they predict correctly? Select enough children to take on each character for a group sculpture. Explain that you are going to focus on how the other characters will react to what he has done. Think about all aspects of the sculpture; positioning, body language, facial expressions, hand gestures. The children watching should move the characters into position around Custard. How can they show the change in feeling towards him?

- Read to 'and her little red wagon' and alter the next line to *'but does she still have her little pet dragon?'* Ask the children to think about Custard. He needs to decide if he should stay with Belinda or move on. Perform a decision alley – reasons to stay and reasons to go. Children share their ideas as a small group of children move through the alley as Custard. At the end ask the 'Custard' group to decide and give their reasons.

- Finally, return to the poem and complete it. Custard is still crying at the end. Did Belinda give him the right name?

The Spider and the Fly

Age range: 5–7 years

What you will need: A copy of *The Spider and the Fly* by Tony Diterlizzi (Simon & Schuster, 2012), and space in class for children to move around.

- Ask the children if they know the poem or what the poem might be about. Talk in pairs about what they know about spiders and flies and how the poem might use this. Explain that this is based on a cautionary tale by Mary Howitt – you may want to discuss what this means.
- Read the poem up to 'I'll snugly tuck you in!' Enlarge and use the images to help the children visualise the characters. Ask children to freeze frame the scene between the spider and the fly at this point. Develop this quickly into a thought tracking exercise, asking children to speak as the characters and say what the characters might be thinking at this stage.
- Read on until you reach the part with the looking glass. Repeat the freeze frames and thought tracking – consider how the thoughts and feelings of the characters have changed. Extend the freeze frames, ask the children to freeze frame what they think will happen next in the poem, giving each frame a heading that shows what is happening.
- Read the next two lines. Discuss what has happened; the fly is leaving. Talk the children on, but the spider is a hungry beast and knows quite well this fly is his only feast. So he follows fast behind the fly, he stops her steps to tell her why she should stay.
- Ask the children to become the spider and the fly and improvise the conversation. How will the spider persuade her to stay? What will the fly do? Move round and collect some ideas from the children to tie back into the poem. Repeat the last few lines then add . . . 'He said . . . ' (add in the ideas from the children). He pleaded for her not to go but in the end she did just so.
- Move back into the poem and read on to the end. Ask the children finally to create a freeze frame to show what they thought the poem was about, again ask for headings. This will enable you to assess how much they have understood of the text.
- Go on to hot seat the characters, asking the ghost of the fly why she went back etc. You could add in a decision alley before she goes back making the children think about her reasons.

Little Red Riding Hood and the Wolf

Age range: 5–7 years

What you will need: A copy of *Little Red Riding Hood and the Wolf* by Roald Dahl (Puffin, 2005).

- Ask children to discuss with a partner what they know about Little Red Riding Hood. Do any of them know different versions? Explain that this poem does not follow the traditional tale completely and you will be looking at the characters and the events through using drama.
- Read the poem up to 'May I come in?'. Ask the children how it differs to the traditional beginning. Continue reading until 'She stopped. She stared.' Get the children into a semi-circle around a chair, ask a confident child or a group of children to be the wolf and sit them down. Get all the other children in role as LRRH. Thought track LRRH. You may need to talk the children back in, repeat the last few lines from the poem and then get them to share what LRRH is thinking. As they do this they can step forward or stay in the circle. An adult may have to demonstrate to encourage them to begin.
- Develop this into small group improvisations, e.g. what could happen next? Get some children to be the wolf and others LRRH who could role play the next scene. Use this time to gather ideas from the children that you can bring back into the text. Talk the children back into the poem using some of their ideas. 'In came the little girl in red. She stopped. She stared. And then she said' (add in children's ideas).
- Read to 'I'm going to eat you anyway!' Freeze frame what happens next. Get children to take a mental photo for the newspaper. Give it a headline.
- Explain that the photographs have been seen by a national paper and they want to interview LRRH (and the wolf if he is still alive in your version!) about what happened. Place children in role as the parts (or you may want to take on the role yourself!); all the other children are reporters. Give the children a chance to talk about how they are going to act and what questions/answers they are going to use. Then hot-seat the characters. Use this to move into writing.

What the Ladybird Heard

Age range: 5–7 years

What you will need: A copy of *What the Ladybird Heard* by Julia Donaldson (MacMillan Children's Books, 2010).

- This delightful story is told in rhyming verse and offers many opportunities for exploring the characters and events through drama.
- Spend time with the front cover. Explore the different textures and spot the flight of the Ladybird.
- Look at the double page spread which shows the farm. Give time for the children to spot as many farm animals as they can. What else do they notice?
- Start reading the story and invite the children to join in with the sounds of the animals.
- Look at the double page with the sounds from the animals. Invite children to play around with the poetic language by re-ordering the lines.
- Possibly give the children cut out strips with the lines on them so they can move about. Ask the children, in their groups, to come up with their own composition.
- Stop at the page where we are told 'And the ladybird said never a word.' Ask the children what the animals might be expecting the ladybird to say. Discuss whether the ladybird has a sound associated with it?
- Read to the point where the ladybird sees and hears the plans of the thieves.
- Tell the children that the ladybird knew that something had to be done so gathered the other farm animals around to share the plan.
- In small groups the children should come up with their plan for saving the farm. You may want to give them the picture of the farm from the start of the book to support their ideas.

Gran Can You Rap?

Age range: 5–7 years

What you will need: A copy of *Gran Can You Rap?* by Jack Ousbey.

- *Gran Can you Rap?* Is a wonderful poem by Jack Ousbey which is guaranteed to bring a smile to the faces of those reading, reciting and performing this poem.
- You may want to start by playing a word association game with the children. You call out a word and the children need to say or write the first word which comes into their minds. End the game with the word Gran, Granma or Granny.
- Gather the results from the class and discuss where their perceptions have come from. Note how you find it fascinating that no one associated a Gran with rapping! Ask the children why that might be?
- Read the poem *Gran Can you Rap?* to the children. Encourage the children to ask questions and make statements about the poem such as:

> I wonder why . . .
> I don't know why . . .
> I think that . . .
> Maybe . . .
> It could be that . . .

- Now ask the children to think of one question they would like to ask Gran.
- Gather the questions together and discuss them as a whole class. Explain that these will be added to as the lesson goes on before being able to actually ask them to Gran!
- In order to become immersed in the poem read it again asking the children to help you with the rhythm by clapping or clicking their fingers.
- Talk to the children about the actions which could accompany the poem. Take feedback and decide on some common actions to use throughout the poem.
- Read the poem again with the class joining in with the rhythm and the actions.

- Children, in their groups, should pick their favourite part of the poem to perform. This could be a whole stanza or part of one. Give the children time and space to enjoy talking about their favourite part and deciding how they will perform it.
- Gather the children together to perform the poem. It will be interesting to see which parts the children enjoyed the most.
- After the performance return to the questions about Gran. Ask the children whether they would like to add any more or take any away which may have been answered through the lesson.
- Explain that the children will be able to ask their questions to Gran in the hot seat.
- Ask the children to consider which questions they would like to ask. They may want to ask from a certain perspective. For example the questions could come from the perspective of an annoyed neighbour, embarrassed relative or a supportive fellow senior citizen.
- Invite two or three children to the hot seat in role as Gran.
- Enjoy the hot seat experience as the children ask and answer questions exploring the character of Gran.

DRAMA AND POETRY FOR KEY STAGE 2

The Highwayman

Age range: 7–11 years

What you will need: A copy of *The Highwayman* by Alfred Noyes and Charles Keeping (OUP Oxford, 2013), a mask or an object the Highwayman might have, large strips of paper, large pens and enough room for groups to work on the floor in the classroom.

There is a lot that can be done with this poem. You can dip in and out of the following ideas or plan extra time to allow enough to move through it as a whole.

- Ask the children if they know what a highwayman is. You may need to explain this before moving forward. This poem has a lot of imagery, some of it will need to be explored as you read through to help children develop an understanding of the plot and characters.
- Read part one of the poem, up to where the highwayman leaves. Ask children to freeze the scene as the highwayman turns his horse and moves away. Get them to freeze frame this scene. Move this into thought tracking get each child to think about what their character is thinking and feeling at this time. Go through each character and ask the children just to voice their ideas out loud, follow this with a short discussion about Tim and how he fits into the poem.
- Read the beginning of part two up to 'though hell shall bar the way!'. Repeat the thought tracking for Bess. Get children to close their eyes and place themselves in Bess' place, what are her thoughts, her fears? Get the children to voice them in turn. Pull these ideas into the text . . . 'as she stood right up to attention, the tears they clouded her eyes as she thought of . . . ' (remember it does not have to rhyme!).
- Read the next verse . . . 'the trigger at least was hers!' At this point we want to deepen our understanding of Bess. Lay out the large paper and provide the children with big pens for them to complete a role on the wall. Get them to draw round a member

of the group. On the inside they can record how Bess is feeling on the outside they can record all of the events that have caused these feelings. Move round the groups and help the children extend their ideas further using open questions.

- Take this on into a freeze frame of what they think will happen next. Then see how close they are, read on. Read up to 'died in the darkness there.' Thought track the highwayman, bring the class into a circle. Place an object that could belong to the highwayman on a chair in the centre. The children become the highwayman, moving in to touch the object as they say how they are feeling or what they are thinking.
- Draw ideas together, explain that the highwayman has a decision to make. Ask the children to sit in small groups and think about what they would do and why. Then form a decision alley, get a small group of children to become the highwayman and as they walk through the alley the others state his thoughts and arguments. 'I should go back because . . . I should run away because . . . '. After this ask the children who played the highwayman to say what they would do after hearing all the ideas.

The Visitor

Age range: 7–11 years

What you will need: A copy of *The Visitor* by Ian Serrailier.

This activity encourages children to explore a narrative poem full of tension and drama. It uses sound and movement to add to the narrative.

- Read the first three lines of the poem. Discuss where the poem is set, what atmosphere is being created? How can we add to the atmosphere? Create a soundscape. What sounds might be heard? The sea, night time creatures, the man's footsteps . . . . Group children and perform a soundscape, reading the lines over and over.
- Read up to 'They slipped off to bed.' Freeze frame the couple and then predict what will happen next, creating another frame.
- Read from 'At midnight . . .' to the second 'It'll soon go away.' Discuss what is happening in the narrative. Thought track the character of the man. What is he thinking/feeling at this point? What does he think it is? Children take it in turns to step into the circle and speak as if they were him.
- Continue to focus on this section. Look at how the poet repeats the lines 'What was that, William? What did it say? Don't worry, my dear. It'll soon go away.' Use this to create a ritual chant. How can the chant be used to build the tension at this point? Perform the chant adding to the atmosphere.
- Continue to read the poem till the end. Discuss the main feelings that run through the poem. Explain that as a class they are going to perform the poem. You can do this in several ways. You, as the teacher, can read the poem while the children add to it with the soundscape and chant. You could also group the children into the different characters and allow them to perform each part. Or you could split the class and do both at the same time.

Mary Celeste

Age range: 7–11 years

What you will need: A copy of *Mary Celeste* by Judith Nicholls.

This activity encourages children to explore a complex narrative poem and the mystery within the plot.

- Explain that this poem is set on an old sailing ship. Ask the children to tell each other what they know about these kinds of ships. Has anyone heard of the Mary Celeste? What do they know?
- Read the first verse to get the children into the feel of the poem and of being on board. Ask them to freeze frame, on their own, an action that might be taking place on the ship at this time. Get them to complete several frames to show different actions, these could be performed to some watery music.
- Read the next verse; the children should become the first mate, thought track him. Say what he is feeling, what would he want to say to his wife, his children? What is he dreaming of? This could lead into writing the letter.
- Read up to 'What drew the captain's cry?' This may need further discussion so the children understand that the people on board have disappeared. Tell them on board was a camera, set up by the sleepless child. She was worried that something might happen so she set it as a trap to help capture any strange goings on. When the ship rolls into harbour and they find the camera's film they develop it. What did they find on the camera? One image? Several? They show what happened that gentle day. Get the children to form a series of freeze frames that show what happened. This could be developed into an improvisation.
- Read the penultimate verse and add the ideas of what might have happened. 'Some say that on this gentle day . . . ' (add the children's ideas) 'but . . . ' then finish with the last verse.

10 Things Found in a Drowned Sailor's Pocket

Age range: 7–11 years

What you will need: A copy of *10 Things Found In a Drowned Sailor's Pocket* by Ian McMillan.

This activity encourages children to explore a range of possibilities relating to objects found in a sailor's pocket.

- Read the poem to the class a couple of times.
- Ian McMillan's poem takes the form of a list. Give groups of children single strips of each line of the poem and ask them put the poem together to create a different order to reflect another way of capturing a possible story of the sailor's life.
- Ask the children to present their poem both orally and on paper, considering the order and orientation of the lines.
- Invite the children, in their groups, to choose one of the lines which interests them.
- Give time and space for the children to consider the significance of the line they have chosen and to think about the importance of the item to the sailor.
- Children should imagine the moment the sailor received the item. Groups are to talk about this moment and the significance of it.
- In groups children could construct a freeze frame of this moment. In order to explore the importance of this moment you could thought track both the sailor and the giver of the item.
- Extend this by asking children to consider what happened before and after this moment. In their groups, children should have time to develop their story by showing the freeze frames before and after this moment.
- Ask the class to compose a new poem based on the 10 things idea. For example: a fairy who has lost her magic; a homeless person; Little Red Riding Hood

What Has Happened to Lulu?

Age range: 7–11 years

What you will need: A copy of *What Has Happened to Lulu?* By Charles Causley.

- This is an emotional poem which explores the themes of loss, grief, growing up, relationships and families and is more appropriate for older children.
- The poem is in the form of a ballad with the second and fourth line of each four-line stanza rhyming. It is a series of questions asked of Lulu's mother probably by a younger sibling.
- Read the poem through a couple of times and invite the class to suggest what might have happened and why? What age do they think Lulu is?
- Suggest to the class that she accidentally left behind a small bag in her room, invite them to draw the items in it and then share their drawings in groups.
- Invite groups to create freeze frames of one or two of the most important items.
- View each these as a class and decide what they reveal about Lulu.
- Invite the children to adopt the position of Lulu in her room the night before she left. What conflicting thoughts are going through her head?
- Read the poem again and then invite the class to voice her thoughts through simultaneous monologues or thought tracking.
- Offer scraps of paper for children to write the note Lulu left, to whom was it addressed?
- As teacher in role sit as mother and invite the children to step forward, read their message and offer it to you. Respond as if you are thinking aloud or speaking directly back to your daughter.
- Look back at the poem and discuss how the poet created this mystery, are there clues as yet unsolved?
- Invite the class to show Lulu some weeks later in freeze frames and to title these. Where is she now? Back home after a holiday? Still at college? Living at nana's?

CHAPTER 4

Exploring non-fiction through drama conventions

This chapter offers the reader 24 ideas to *Jumpstart! Drama* in relation to non-fiction oral texts, albeit these may arise from fictional contexts. Focusing on non-fiction text types, these ideas will enable the reader to not only identify reading and writing opportunities but will also generate a range of purposeful speaking and listening. Linking to the drama conventions outlined in chapter 1 the reader will be able to recognise how non-fiction can be explored through a range of fictitious worlds.

DRAMA AND RECOUNTS

The lost bear

Age range: 5–7 years:

What you will need: A copy of *This Is the Bear* by Sarah Hayes (Walker Books, 2003) (or a book with a simple progression of events) plain paper and pencils.

- Look at the cover of the text; ask the children in pairs to discuss what might happen in the story.
- Read the text through to the children.
- Group children in twos or threes and ask them to recount the main events. Ask them to choose three or four events they think are important and create freeze frames to show them.
- Create a timeline on the board and identify missing events they think are important.

- Make sure each group has one event from the timeline. Ask them to create a silent improvisation of that event.
- Read the story (or tell it if you feel confident), allowing the children to add their improvisation when appropriate.
- To extend this activity the children could add events to the recount and tell different versions of the story.
- This could lead into a simple diary entry from the bear.

Newsnight

Age range: 5–7 years

What you will need: Large TV cutout or newsdesk; images of recent news reports.

This activity invites the children to take on news presenter roles, recounting events either real or imagined.

- Talk about the news and that it can be found in written and visual form. Explain that they are going to be creating a news program recounting various stories of interest.
- Give children a selection of images to choose from. Ask each child to choose one and recount what might have happened with a partner. Use this stage to remind children of features of a recount.
- Group children into threes and ask them to pick one of the pictures that could provide an interesting story. The group should then plan an improvisation of the event. They should then take it further using a broadcaster to add a verbal recount.
- With the teacher in role as the newsreader, the whole class can take part in a news program with the teacher linking between the different outside broadcasts. The children can then use these ideas for their writing.

Story adventures

Age range: 7–11 years

What you will need: A copy of *The Snow Dragon* by Vivian French (Picture Corgi Books, 2000); a digital camera and large sheets of paper.

This activity involves children recounting the events of part of a story. There are many stories you could use with this activity but it works well if the characters are off on an adventure.

- Read the story *The Snow Dragon* up to the point when the Fire Dragon is told a Twoleg will defeat him.
- Ask the children, in small groups, to freeze frame what the Fire Dragon might do to the Twolegs. Weave their ideas into the story and continue.
- Read to when he opens the door. Talk the children back up to this point and create a group sculpture of what can be seen behind the door. Place some children in as the character of Little Tuft and thought track the character and how he feels at this point in the story.
- Read to the point when Little Tuft goes off to find the Snow Dragon. At this point the character goes on a long and dangerous journey. Ask the children to discuss in small groups what he might face.
- Each group should then create a series of freeze frames to show the events of the journey. Perform these to each other and photograph. Use these to structure a recount of what took place on the journey. Add some into the original text.

A real life story

Age range: 7–11 years

What you will need: A copy of Malala's *Magic Pencil* by Malala Yousafzai (Puffin, 2017); large sheets of paper and coloured pens.

This activity is based on the text *Malala's Magic Pencil*, a picture book based on the real life events of Malala Yousafzai, the youngest-ever recipient of the Nobel Peace Prize. It can be used to write a formal biography or lead into autobiographical writing.

- Read the story up to 'a proper ball . . .'. Ask children to freeze frame what they would use a magic pencil for.
- Read the following page and create a group sculpture of the children at the dump and Malala. Ask the children to express the thoughts of each character. Read the next page and move into thought tracking Malala.
- Read story up to 'I thought, they might help.' What has happened? How must she feel? How would they feel? Use a large piece of paper and an outline of a person to complete a role on the wall for Malala. Use different colours to record events that have happened and feelings/thoughts.
- Read through the rest of the text – adding to the events/thoughts and feelings.
- Invite the children to hot seat a group of children in role as Malala. Ensure they have all of the events and use this information to write a biography of her.

DRAMA AND EXPLANATIONS

A plan of action

Age range: 5–7 years

What you will need: A copy of *Leaf* by Sandra Dieckmann (Flying Eye Books, 2017).

This activity asks the children to prepare a verbal explanation.

- Read the text up to 'no one was brave enough to talk to him.' Add to the text; explain the animals of the forest called a meeting to discuss the stranger. With teacher in role as leader of the meeting, get the children to become the animals and explain how they are feeling about the stranger. What are they scared of? What do they think should happen?
- Read up to Leaf returning to his cave. Thought track Leaf. What is he doing and why? How is he feeling about being in the forest? Continue the story to the second meeting of the forest animals. Some of the animals are changing how they feel – perform a decision alley – Should they help Leaf?
- Read up to where Leaf explains why he is there and that he is trying to get home. In role as the leader as the animals of the forest get into groups and come up with a plan to get Leaf back to his family. Each group presents their idea, explaining their plan. Extend this by asking children to perform freeze frames of each part of the plan.

How does your garden grow?

Age range: 5–7 years

What you will need: A copy of *The Flower* by John Light (Child's Play Books, 2006); a range of research books and various seed packets.

This activity stems from a text called *The Flower* as its stimulus. The children need to know or have time to research how plants grow.

- Read the text up to the point when the character finds the seeds. Teacher as storyteller leads the children to explain that he does not know what they are or how to use them but he is desperate to find out. He looks back at his forbidden book to see how he can turn these crinkled specks into beautiful flowers. When he opens his book it magically springs to life.
- Explain to the children that they are going to be the book and explain to Brigg how to get flowers from his seeds.
- With the teacher as narrator lead the children through using linking phrases. First . . . then . . . following that . . . . As the teacher narrates the children create a freeze frame on their own to show the action or process.
- Talk about which frames worked and why. Ask children to review and improve their frames to make it really clear. Then perform the explanation as a class.

New inventions

Age range: 7–11 years

What you will need: A copy of *Until I Met Dudley* by Roger McGough and Chris Riddell (Frances Lincoln, 2012); a digital camera, images of everyday objects and large paper.

- Look at pages from the text, focus on the imaginative explanations rather than the real.
- Place the children into small groups and give them an everyday object.
- Ask the groups to come up with an idea of how the object works. They should then create freeze frames of the object working in different stages.
- After the children have worked on their freeze frames photograph them.
- Ask the children to organize the photographs into the working order and glue them onto a large sheet of paper.
- Using the board the children should explain verbally how their object works. This could be to the class or another group.
- To extend this let them group write the explanation.
- You could extend this by asking them to then create the real explanation for the object.

Tadpoles and butterflies

Age range: 7–11 years

What you will need: A copy of *Tadpole's Promise* by Jeanne Willis and Tony Ross (Anderson Press, 2005); enlarged copies of the illustrations or photographs showing frog/butterfly life cycle, cameras, and large sheets of paper.

This activity can be conducted as part of a science lesson.

- Read the text. It is a funny/sad story but ask the children where we can get factual information about life cycles from it.
- Group children and give them the images to support. Ask the children to create a diagram of the life cycle of the frog using their bodies.
- The children should be given time to discuss and refine their ideas. They will need to frame or role play the sections of their game to illustrate how the frog changes. These can either be photographed or videoed, depending on the outcome wanted.
- The children should then prepare a script or written explanation to accompany the visual elements. They may choose to complete as a TV documentary.
- These should then be performed to a different class or group. Use the butterfly cycle if you need a shorter explanation.

DRAMA AND INSTRUCTIONS

Instructions brought to life

Age range: 5–7 years

What you will need: The school camera and card for writing the instructions.

This activity involves the whole class in creating a physical instructional board to show the sequential process of making something. Take photos of the sequence and add instructions appropriate to each freeze frame to make a display.

- Discuss with the class the order and set of instructions for your chosen focus: this might involve making an emergency phone call, pumping up a bicycle tyre, planting seeds, making a sandwich etc.
- Explain to the class that together you are going to make freeze frames of the ingredients/resources needed and each of the steps in the process and that you will take photographs of their freeze frames, to make a display/poster showing the process.
- Allocate to each group of three to five children one of the resources needed or one part of the process and ask them to construct a freeze frame or a mime of their part. Some may be using their bodies to create slices of bread, or shape a jar of pickles, whilst others may be demonstrating cutting the cheese.
- As teacher in role, as a cookery advisor or a road safety instructor (as appropriate to the instruction) talk through the instructions watching as a class as each group shows its visual of the resources or stage of the process.
- Take a photo of each group and then invite the groups to write a sentence to go with their visual.
- Display these photos as a poster or wall display with their accompanying instructions.

Blue Peter

Age range: 5–7 years

What you will need: copies of children's magazines and comics, and the simple resources associated with the craft instructions in them. Or your own craft instructions and resources. A large cardboard box/ sheet of hard card cut out to create a TV screen with a large gap in the middle.

This activity involves the class selecting a craft activity, making it and then presenting it on their own *Blue Peter* show, sharing their ready-made versions and offering instructions to children nationwide who wish to make the item.

- Explain to the class they can choose in pairs to work on a making activity from those available.
- Explain that they are going to have the chance to present the programme instructions for their making activity on *Blue Peter*.
- When the pairs have made their . . . pop up puppets, finger puppets, and so forth, allow time for them to practice the presentation of this as a piece of prepared improvisation complete with resources needed and the instructional process and the chance to share the one they made earlier.
- Set up the TV screen and over time give the pairs the chance to perform as a planned improvisation an extract from *Blue Peter*.
- You could appear as Teacher in Role as a current *Blue Peter* host and introduce each pair as experts in the making of puppets and so forth.
- Discuss the presenters work and perhaps reflect upon the differences and similarities between the oral and the written genre.

Great British bake off!

Age range: 7–11 years

What you will need: a chocolate Swiss roll, icing sugar, weighing scales, tablespoons, a sieve, a large silver cake board and Yuletide decorations and a table from which to demonstrate.

This activity involves the teacher adopting the role of a famous celebrity chef, such as Paul Hollywood, Mary Berry or Prue Leith from the Great British bake off and demonstrating a simple baking recipe; this one involves decorating a Yule Log.

- Invite the children to become writers preparing materials for the BBC Good Food website, you might even check out this or other food websites with them to discuss the layout and the presentation of these instructional texts.
- As teacher in role introduce yourself to the children as the celebrity chef and welcome them as BBC writers to the demonstration session, explain you are going to demonstrate a recipe for decorating a Chocolate Yule Log.
- Hand out whiteboards or paper and invite them to record the process making it clear that visitors to the website will want simple and direct instructions.
- In role as the famous chef, slowly but with panache undertake the process, talking aloud what ingredients you need and the process of weighing and then sifting the sugar, adding cocoa powder and water and decorating the cake to make the it look like a log. Finally, show them how to add a robin, holly leaves and other decorations.
- Having made notes they could write up the final version.
- This acts as a good assessment exercise to assess their knowledge of organisation and structure of procedural texts.
- Later the children could then decorate their own Yule Logs in groups or take the recipe home, or at least least could be placed on the school website.

Art Ninja

Age range: 7–11 years

What you will need: the resources for six art and craft Christmas activities, these might include e.g. making Christmas crackers, snowflakes for the windows, chains of joined up snowmen, paper lanterns and paper chains.

This activity involves the class in groups in presenting to each other the oral instructions for different art activities, these could be related to a given theme – crafts related to Easter, Mother's day or Christmas (as in this example) or maybe a series of individual craft activities or a science focus . Afterwards you could invite the class in groups to present the instructions for their artwork or science experiments.

- Explain to the class that as they create their Christmas crafts they need to make a note of the process, order and details involved so that they can present this to others in an *Art Ninja* programme and offer an accompanying instruction leaflet.
- Watch a brief extract from *Art Ninja* to remind the class of this programme and to notice the oral features of the instructional genre.
- Engage the children in groups in different arts and crafts activities, revisiting well known activities that have made before. Do not provide them with detailed instructions, but make available the resources they need. Each group makes the item and produces a leaflet to describe the process.
- Offer time for their *Art Ninja* work as prepared improvisations; ensure all members of each groups are involved in presenting some aspect of their item on the programme.
- Set up the room so that each group present on the TV show, teaching the rest of the class how to make a Christmas cracker e.g. the class can review which presentation was the most organised and interesting.
- Groups then choose which activity they would like to make and, using the presenters' leaflets, follow the instructions and construct these. Build in time to review the instructional leaflets.

DRAMA AND PERSUASION

The Rainbow Fish

Age range: 5–7 years

What you will need: A copy of *The Rainbow Fish* by Marcus Pfeiffer (North-South, 2007).

This activity involves the whole class in adopting roles as sea creatures in the ocean and trying to persuade the rainbow fish who is teacher in role to share his beautiful rainbow coloured and possibly magical scales. The same persuasive conversation is initially developed in pairs to enable the children to generate ideas to use later in the whole class improvisation.

- Discuss the front cover of the book with the children- point out the Rainbow Fish's beautiful shiny scales.
- Read the start of the book to the point at which the Rainbow Fish meets the starfish and wonders what to do – should he share his scales?
- Explain to the class that that night the little fish returned to try and persuade the Rainbow Fish to share his scales – he so badly wanted one to lighten up his cave, to keep him warm – to make him famous perhaps . . . . Invite the children to undertake pairs role play: one is the Rainbow Fish, the other the little fish – ask them what other ideas they might have for using one of the scales and ponder aloud whether the RF will be tempted.
- Share ideas offered and then narrate a short story about how the next day a number of cod, lobsters, eels, starfish, sharks and other sea creatures gathered together to discuss the problem. Invite the class to brainstorm such creatures and select one, moving around the class as a crab, for example and thinking how to persuade the Rainbow Fish.
- As teacher in role, you can become the wise old Octopus and invite all the creatures to a meeting to share their ideas with you. Listen to some of these, asking the fish to state who they are, e.g. a seahorse and their idea to persuade the Rainbow Fish.

- Narrate that as they were meeting the Rainbow Fish happened upon the creatures. Using a colourful scarf to denote this is now you – 'swim' towards them and ask what they are meeting about. A whole class improvisation will unfold from here with the creatures trying to persuade you to share your scales.
- It will be important to defend your previous decision – perhaps your deceased parents gave you the scales – perhaps you'd be in pain if some were removed– perhaps a compromise may be reached– do NOT be tied to the story, you are creating your own version with the class.

Dogger

Age range: 5–11 years

What you will need: A copy of *Dogger* by Shirley Hughes (Red Fox, 2009).

This activity involves the class in two persuasive conversations in role: one when Alfie loses Dogger, his beloved soft toy dog (he needs to persuade mum and dad to go out in the dark and search for him) and later in the tale when Alfie sees a little girl has bought Dogger at the school fete (he wants to persuade her to give/sell it to him). Both activities could lead to writing in Alfie's diary or a note to mum/the girl.

- Read the story to the point at which Alfie cannot find Dogger. He does not know where he lost his toy. Suggest that mum is tired, needs to get the tea and does not want to go out in the dark and hunt but that Alfie desperately does. Invite them to pair up as Alfie and mum and see if they can persuade their mother.
- Ask the class if any of their arguments persuaded mum and take up teacher in role as dad and see if the class as Alfie can persuade you to find a torch and take him hunting for Dogger.
- Read some more of the book until the point when Alfie sees Dogger at the school fete and watches in despair as the little girl buys him. Can he persuade her? Invite the class to undertake paired role play again, swapping roles so that one is Alfie and one the girl.
- List some ideas which Alfie might put forward and any ideas the class have for negotiating or bargaining with the girl. These might be noted on the IWB and then with half the class as the girl and half as Alfie revisit the role play making use of these ideas.
- Complete the reading of the book and discuss the option Shirley Hughes chose. Compare this with their ideas.

Rats!

Age range: 7–11 years

What you will need: A copy of *Rats!* by Pat Hutchins (Red Fox, 1991).

This activity involves the class in a role play from the start of the book when Sam, unbeknown to his parents, sees a rat in a pet shop, purchase and pays for it and arranges with the lady he will pick it up on Monday. The role play involves the class in pairs, in small groups, as half and half and working with the teacher in role as Sam trying to persuade his mother to let him keep it. It could be undertaken to promote the book for independent reading or to commence class reading of this hilarious novel.

- Read the opening chapter to the point at which Sam is trying to persuade his mother he can have a rat.
- Ask the children, to engage in paired role play as mum and Sam and see whether mum can be persuaded. Partner yourself with a child and be sure to be Sam.
- Judge the moment to interrupt and suggest the children gather in groups of four, with two role playing Sam and two in role as Mum. You may need to model this with one group to ensure they grasp that two people are representing one person.
- Ask the children about the basis of Sam's persuasive argument. Is he lonely? Does he need a friend? Does he want to be a vet? Does he want to be like his friends/brother? Record their ideas on the board. Discuss how he might persuade mum, both perhaps through his arguments and some negotiation? Record additional ideas.
- Ask half the class to stand as Mum, hands on hips and half to stand as Sam, facing her and desperate. Begin a whole class role play challenging the class to make explicit use of the various persuasive arguments and points of negotiation listed.
- The children could commit this persuasive argument to paper or screen in the style of the text.

The Lonely Beast

Age range: 7–11 years

What you will need: a copy of the book *The Lonely Beast* by Chris Judge (Anderson Press, 2011).

- Read the book until the page when he arrives in the city and everyone runs away
- Invite the class to construct in groups the Lonely Beast lying down at the edge of the city somewhere that night – they can use their bodies or furniture, clothing and anything to hand.
- Invite them to develop an inner monologue for the Beast, a repetitive refrain which kept running through his head.
- With the class look at each one in turn and listen to the Beasts sighs and his refrain.
- Ask them to predict what might happen if the Beast stays there?
- Invite groups to make freeze frames of something that terrible that happened a few days later.
- Watch each of these and discuss what happened.
- Narrate their ideas into a series of events that befell the Beast in the city and stress his loneliness, then suggest that some children came to talk to him as they felt sorry for him.
- Divide the class in half, one side faces the other, half are the beast and half the children, can the children persuade the Beast that humans can be trusted and that he can stay and will be safe now? Listen to all arguments.
- Read on in the book until the Beast appears on TV, in pairs invite children to role play the Beast and the TV presenter.
- Read to the close of the book.
- Return to the persuasive arguments offered to the Beast, although he stayed for a while these arguments didn't work – discuss why?
- Invite the class to create small group sculptures of the key message of the text with a title.
- Look at each sculpture in turn with the rest of the class and discuss your collective interpretation of them.

DRAMA AND REPORTS

A new species

Age range: 5–7 years:

What you will need: A copy of *The Gruffalo* by Julia Donaldson and Axel Scheffle (Macmillan Children's Books, 2017); large sheets of paper, pens, card strips.

This activity is based on a very well-known book *The Gruffalo* by Julia Donaldson and Axel Scheffler; Macmillan. It uses the description within the story to create a report for *National Geographic*.

- Read the story through. Talk in pairs about the main events in the story.
- Group children and give them one of the parts from the first section of the story, e.g. meeting the fox. Each group takes on part of the story, performing in role as Mouse and Fox etc.
- Perform each part but get the group to freeze the action just as the animals leave. Ask each of the Foxes to verbalise how they are feeling and why they are feeling that way. Repeat for the other animals.
- Discuss why the animals are scared of the Gruffalo, what do we know about him? Interview the characters to collect information on appearance, diet etc. Record ideas onto cards. Group ideas into sections and use these to structure the written report.

Big blue

Age range: 5–7 years

What you will need: A copy of *Big Blue Whale* by Nicola Davies (Walker, 2015); large whale outline, big pens, large paper and other items the children may use in their report.

This activity is based on the text *Big Blue Whale* by Nicola Davies (Walker, 2015). The book provides the children with some knowledge on which they can base a simple report about the blue whale.

- Read *Big Blue Whale*, explain that as it is read the children will need to try and hold onto factual information for their report.
- Give children one minute to discuss things they have remembered about whales from the story. Ask them to then record in images or simple words on the whale – an adult could scribe the facts they now know.
- Group children and explain that they will be giving a presentation on the whale to the class. Ask them to think about the main areas they would include in their report. One or two should be the presenters while the others will create an improvisation. They should create a series of freeze frame images, the children may choose to make these come to life. The presenters can then report on what is taking place.
- Perform to the class and reflect on each other's work.

Picture this!

Age range: 7–11 years

What you will need: Enlarged sentences or paragraphs from a report split into different sections.

This activity involves children becoming part of a non-chronological report. You can choose to make a report about any subject.

- Tell the children they are going to create a living book report. Split them into groups and give each group a section of the report to work on. Explain they must read the section and identify what it is about.
- They must then organize themselves into a freeze frame (or a number of frames if dealing with a larger extract) that informs the viewer about the text and possible offers further detail.
- The children should then present these to each other in groups or as a class. They must then try and work out an order for the text and the visual images.
- Once an order has been established they should perform the report, reading the text as they go from one frame to the next.
- This can be extended with the children writing their own sections for the images or creating a text from scratch.

Sky One documentary

Age range: 7–11 years

What you will need: Space for groups to work, books on animals for the children to use as part of their research.

This activity involves the children creating short improvisations based on factual knowledge of a subject area. Animals are always a good base for report construction as it has clear elements that the children can structure their report on.

- Explain to the children they will be creating a short documentary program about a particular animal. The documentary will be presented by the teacher and the children will provide the wildlife features.
- Warm up by asking the children to think of an animal they know well. Ask them to improvise an act that that animal would do, repeat so the children have several different actions. e.g. eat, move, clean etc.
- Group the children and ask them to choose an animal for the show to include. They should then create several shots, improvisations that display how that animal lives.
- Invite each group to perform their section whilst teacher in role acts as a presenter, reporting on the events that are taking place.
- This could then be taken further, with the groups including more detail in their sections and the children themselves becoming the presenters providing the report.

DRAMA AND DISCUSSION

The bear and the scary night

Age range: 5–7 years

What you will need: A copy of *This is the Bear and the Scary Night* by Sarah Hayes and Helen Craig (Walker Books, 2003).

This activity involves the whole class in initially listening to the story and then creating a series of small group freeze frames to denote the stages of the story and then examining in more detail the thoughts of the Bear once he is safely home. It provides an opportunity for the children to consider the multiple perspectives on his adventures through the eyes of the bear as he tells the rest of the toys in the nursery about his 'scary night'.

- Read the story and invite the class to make a big still picture of the tale with their bodies.
- Read it again and this time allocate a double page spread to each small group of children (approx. 3–4). Each group will be creating a freeze frame e.g. of the bear being rescued by the man with the slide trombone.
- Give the children time to make their freeze frames and then read the book a third time slowly. As you come to each page the groups of children show their freeze frame for that page, whilst the rest watch. In effect the class is making a physical storyboard.
- Narrate that when the bear got back to the boy's bedroom and the boy had gone to supper all the other toys gathered round the bear desperate to hear about his night out. Half the toys seemed to think it was the scariest night ever with sharp clawed owls, falling from the sky and the possibility of drowning, but the rest saw it as an exciting adventure – like going on a funfair!
- Ask the children to decide which view they take and arrange so the like-minded toys sit together in two groups.
- You are the bear as teacher in role, explain this to them and tell your friends the toys that you are thinking of venturing out in

the night and are hoping for more adventures, but you're not sure. Ask them to help you decide and examine together the pros and cons of this – leading into a discussion.

- To close the drama you could share your decision to go or stay at home.

The tooth fairy

Age range: 5–7 years

What you will need: A copy of *Horrid Henry Tricks the Tooth Fairy* by Francesca Simon (Orion, 1997).

This activity involves the teacher in reading from the book and enabling the class to explore the behaviour of Horrid Henry, who badly wants money from the tooth fairy and tries to trick her. It involves role play both in pairs and as a whole class with teacher in role as Henry and the class as his mother or father.

- Read chapter 1 to when Henry, having tried to eat sweets to prompt a tooth loss, frustrated at his brother Peter's successful loss of a tooth, steals it at night and puts it under his pillow.
- Invite the class in twos to adopt roles as Henry's parents who are fairly sure that Henry has stolen it and discuss what to do. Should they leave the money under Peter's pillow? Should they leave Henry a note? Should they remove the tooth from Henry's pillow? Consider their options aloud and if the class is not used to role play, model this with one child, with you as teacher in role as one of his parents and the child as the other.
- Explain to the class that as Henry goes to bed he overhears his parents' conversation, and then explain you are going to walk around the class as Henry and listen in to their discussions of what to do about their naughty son. Listen into a selection allowing each pair to share 30 seconds of their discussion.
- Read on to when his mother finds Henry has eaten all the sweets. In pairs again invite the class to role play Henry's response to his mother's anger.
- Complete the short story and adopt the role of mother/father inviting the class to adopt the alternative role. Then with teacher in role prompt a discussion with your partner about Henry, drawing on his behaviour in other stories too which the class knows. In effect you are creating a whole class discussion.

King of the Sky

Age range: 7–11 years

What you will need: a copy of *King of the Sky* by Nicola Davies and Laura Carlin (Walker Books, 2017).

This activity involves reading a Key Stage Two picture book to the class and stopping at various points to examine and discuss the plight and perspective of the boy. You may want to refer to the points presented in the role play section for additional ideas.

- Read the book to the line "All if it told me / This is not where you belong"
- Invite the children to discuss in pairs if they've ever felt as if they didn't fit in, weren't sure they wanted to be where they were, felt displaced in some way . . .
- Re-read the book this far and invite them to adopt positions as the boy leaning soulfully against the door frame. Invite everyone to simultaneously voice aloud their thinking
- Read on to introduce Mr Evans and the naming of the pigeon King of the Sky. Invite the class in pairs to role play either Mr Evans telling his wife that night or the boy telling his mother.
- Listen to a few snippets of these – discuss what more you all know about the characters though this dramatic creation
- Read on until "I waited two whole days and nights but the pigeon with the milk white head did not return". Invite the class to voice interior monologues as the boy at this point.
- Adopting the role of mother interrupt them and tease out why he is so down, how can he be sure it will not return, has he no faith in the bird, will his nana not have fed the bird and sent him back ?
- Read to the end of the text.
- Invite the class in groups to create a group sculpture with their bodies which conveys the key message of the text as they see it and title it. Also explain the material it's made from e.g. have included a circle of flagpoles called 'One Earth' and two pebbles called 'One friend is all you need'.
- Take time to discuss these and connect to the text and check out Nicola Davies writing about the book.

Holes

Age range: 7–11 years

What you will need: A copy of *Holes* by Louis Sachar (Bloomsbury Children's Books, 2015).

This activity involves the class in creating an imaginary scenario at the start of the novel *Holes*. This explores the debatable rationale for forcing young people in a prison context to dig holes in the hot sun and involves the class in a whole class improvisation which explores the issues around this form of punishment in the context of the text. It could be used as an introduction to the book which children may then be motivated to read independently or could be used when the novel is being read aloud to the class.

- Read the opening chapter to the part where Stanley arrives at Camp Green Lake and meets Mr Sir.
- Narrate that the following day a group of journalists unexpectedly arrived to interview the staff (and the newest inmate?). Rumours had spread about the enforced labour and poor living conditions.
- Make a list of who might attend the conference. Had a press officer alerted a health official or NSPCC expert? Who from the camp would attend?
- Invite the class to generate possible press questions in pairs. Are they suspicious of maltreatment? What of children's rights? What angle or scoop are they after?
- Invite two to three children and/or the teaching assistant to join you in role as Mr Sir, the Warden, the Camp doctor etc. As teacher in role you will be one of the management, talk with the group about the management's position. In preparation for the conference prompt the rest of the class to record two interesting questions, perhaps about nutrition, education, labour and so on.
- Set up the whole class improvisation by moving furniture so that the Camp team faces the Press.
- As teacher in role welcome the Press making allusions perhaps to your surprise at their sudden arrival. Assure them you run a good penitentiary, of which you are proud, that ensures the boys learn

the value of hard work and recognise the error of their ways. Invite their questions to your team.

- Close the proceedings by thanking the visitors and summarising life at the Camp from your perspective.
- The pros and cons of such a punishment for teenagers could be listed and writing in role might follow.

CHAPTER 5
Developing role play areas

This chapter offers the reader 16 ideas to *Jumpstart! Drama* through role play areas. Role play areas are a crucial opportunity to create imaginary worlds and learn though living in them. Some may be aligned with real world contexts, such as shops, garden centres or vets whereas others may be fictions, such as Miss Wobble the Waitress' café or Percy the park keeper's greenhouse, whilst still others may be entirely fictional, such as castles, caves and little cottages in the wood, in which any adventures may happen . . . .

A LIGHTHOUSE

Based on *The Lighthouse Keeper's Lunch* by Ronda Armitage (Scholastic, 2008).

Resources
Lighthouse cut out (may be left blank for children to design or add to), rope and pulley with basket, row boat, telescope, binoculars, life jackets, Wellington boots, woolly hat, sunglasses, food items, maps of coastlines, circuit making equipment, building materials, walkie-talkies, radio, tidal information.

Characters
Mr Grinling and Mrs Grinling

Lighthouse visitors

Sailors

Rescue teams

Villagers

Predicaments

Mr Grinling loses his lunch to the seagulls; can we find other ways to prevent the gulls from eating the food?

The light stops working on a stormy evening

A large ship crashes into the rocks

Lighthouse Keeper gets stranded when his row boat gets swept away

Lighthouse Keeper takes a holiday and needs a replacement

Teacher in role

A villager to tell the lighthouse keeper that the light is not working and that there are ships close to the rocks

Captain of a ship that is in trouble contacts light house

The Lighthouse Keeper's wife reporting that her husband has not returned home

Texts

The Lighthouse Keeper's Cat by Ronda Armitage

(Scholastic, 2008)

The Lighthouse Keeper's Catastrophe, by Ronda Armitage

(Scholastic, 2014)

The Lighthouse Keeper's Picnic by Ronda Armitage

(Scholastic, 2014)

Lighthouses for Kids by Kath L House

(Chicago Review Press, 2008)

Seaside poems by Jill Bennett

(Oxford University Press, 2006)

Writing

Safety signs for inside the lighthouse

Sandwich recipe cards

Plans to keep the lunch intact

Instructions for building a circuit to run the lighthouse

Newspaper reports of the storm or the ship crash

Incident report on the missing Lighthouse Keeper

A SPACESHIP

Based on *Man on the Moon* by Simon Bartram (Templar Publishing, 2004).

Resources
Rocket shaped tent or foil/card for the outside of the spaceship, space suits, helmets, space boots/wellies, oxygen tanks, control panel with levers and buttons, models of planets, pictures of aliens, pieces of rock collected from different planets, phrases in alien languages, camera, radio to talk to people on Earth, telescope/binoculars, back pack for exploring planets, fairy lights or night light, torch, telescope, binoculars, timer/clock

Characters
Astronauts

Ground crew to launch the rocket

Aliens

Space tourists

Billy, the man on Mars

Sam, the man on Saturn

Communications crew to talk to the people in the rocket

Predicaments
Rocket makes emergency landing and astronauts discover a new planet

Aliens contact the spaceship

There is a problem with the spaceship and it's stranded in space

A space storm throws the spaceship off course and it gets lost

Another spaceship is found floating in space with no one on board

Teacher in role

Contact spaceship from control room on Earth to give directions to a new planet

A new astronaut in training

Captain of an alien space ship wanting to land on the moon

Pilot of a spaceship navigating through a meteor storm

An astronaut preparing to leave the spaceship for a spacewalk

Texts

How to Catch a Star by Oliver Jeffers

(HarperCollins, 2015)

Bob's Lunar Adventures by Simon Bartram

(Templar, 2017)

Space Dog by Mini Grey

(Alfred A. Knopf Books for Young Readers, 2016)

Space Ace by Eric Brown

(Barrington Stoke Ltd, 2017)

Space by Rob Lloyd Jones

(Usborne, 2012)

Aliens Love Underpants by Claire Freedman

(Simon & Schuster Ltd, 2011)

Cosmic Disco by Grace Nichols

(Frances Lincoln Publishers Ltd, 2011)

Whatever Next by Jill Murphy

(Macmillan Children's books, 2018)

Beegu by Alexis Deacon

(Random House Children's Publishers UK, 2004)

Writing
Warning signs for inside the spaceship

Instructions on how to fly a spaceship

Diary or log book of space travel

Alien phrase books

Labels for the control panel in the spaceship

Map of the solar system with directions to different planets

Information about aliens and planets

A CAFÉ

Based on *Mrs Wobble the Waitress* by Alan Ahlberg (Penguin, 1989).

Resources
Tables, chairs and stools, table cloths, napkins, cutlery, salt and pepper, menu holders, a till, kitchen area, stove, cooking materials, telephone and notepad, notice boards.

Characters
Waitresses and waiters

Chefs

People to serve customers

Cleaners

Customers

Delivery people

Person to operate till

Predicaments
Customers complaining about spilt food on clothes

Menus have not arrived in time for the grand opening

Mrs Wobble stops wobbling; will guests still come?

The dishwasher leaks, a flood of water seeps towards the main café

A power cut

Café runs out of chips

The chef is ill

Something is wrong with the food, e.g. too cold

Teacher in role
Journalist to interview the famous juggling waiters

A mother who wants to book a children's themed birthday party

Mr and Mrs Wobble are poorly; who can cook?

Texts
This is the Bear and the Bad Little Girl by Sarah Hayes (Walker, 1994)

Kia's Baking by Sara Lewis (Hamlyn, 2006)

Mr Wolf and the Three Bears by Jan Fearnley (Egmont, 2004)

Writing
Menus

Notepads for food orders

Receipts

Sandwich boards and notices

Adverts and posters for the café

Price list

A CIRCUS

Based on *The Greatest Show on Earth* by John Prater (Candlewick, 1995).

Resources
Colourful striped materials to create big tent feel, box of clothes, face paints, juggling balls, skipping ropes, top hat, bench, P.E mat, balance boards, hoops, bean bags.

Characters
Ring master

The family from the book

Clowns, acrobats and other circus performers

Visitors to the circus

Animals

Predicaments
An animal escapes or is ill

No food is delivered for the big animals

High wire or trapeze is broken

Tent falls down in a storm

There is a hole in the tent and it's started to rain

Clown can't find a costume

Ringmaster loses their voice

Teacher in role
Clown needs cheering up and new ideas for his act

Vet comes to treat one of the ill animals

Strong man is ill; which act can replace his tonight?

Mayor visits; is the circus wanted? The family have to defend their show

Owner needs to convince best acrobat not to leave

Texts
Clown by Quentin Blake

(Red Fox, 1998)

The Dancing Frog by Quentin Blake

(Red Fox, 1996)

Leon and the Place Inbetween by Grahame Baker-Smith

(Templar, 2009)

The Circus Ship by Chris Van Dusen

(Candlewick Press, 2009)

Writing
Posters to advertise the show

Programmes for the show with times of each act

Training routines for the acrobats

Instructions on how to look after the animals

Instructions on how to juggle

Tickets for the show

A BAKERY

Based on *Betty's Burgled Bakery* by Travis Nichols (Chronical books, 2017).

Resources
Counter, till, shelves, oven, baking trays, model food, play dough, bakery tools/equipment, scales, packaging, bags, money, phone, blackboard, order pads and pens, hair nets/bakers hats, aprons, detective badges, note pads and pencils, fingerprint dust

Characters
Bakers

People to serve customers

Cleaners

Customers

Delivery people

Person to operate till

(Detectives and thieves)

Predicaments
Someone has burgled the bakery and stolen everything

The bakery runs out of flour

Mice are found in the kitchen

All the bread gets burned

The age-old book of secret bakery recipes gets dropped in the sink

Teacher in role
A detective called in to interview suspects of the break-in

A customer that is cross about the burnt bread

A baker that has forgotten how to bake a cake

A Health Inspector come to check the bakery

Texts

Biscuit Bear by Mini Grey

(Red Fox Picture Books, 2005)

Master Bun the Baker's Boy by Allen Ahlberg

(Puffin, 1988)

Kids' Baking by Sara Lewis

(Hamlyn, 2003)

Writing

Notepads for orders

Receipts

Sandwich boards and notices

Adverts and posters for the bakery

Price list

Detective reports

Newspaper reports

THE GARDEN

Based on *There's a Tiger in the Garden* by Lizzy Stewart (Frances Lincoln, 2016).

Resources

Artificial grass, soil, flowers, plants (check for dangers around children), images of animals, insects and birds, garden tools, bird house, cameras, binoculars, magnifying glasses

Characters

Gardener

Visitors

Animals that can speak

Predicaments

A massive hole has been dug in the middle of the lawn

All the flowers have been picked and taken in the night

Strange footprints in the flowerbeds

The animals begin to grow

Teacher in role

Gardener who has lost his prize-winning vegetable

The girl/boy who finds a magical world within the long grass

A bird whose tree is being chopped down

A vet who has come to capture an injured fox

Texts

The Secret Path by Nick Butterworth

(HarperCollins, 2011)

The Tiny Seed by Eric Carle

(Puffin, 1997)

The Boy Who Lost His Bumble by Trudi Esbergerm

(Child's Play Ltd, 2014)

Ready, Steady, Grow! by The Royal Horticultural Society

(Dorling Kindersley, 2010)

Writing

Signs for plants

Plant information cards

Instructions for growing

Reports on animals or plants

Posters on how to help the environment

Instructions: how to build a bug hotel

AT THE SEASIDE

Based on *Come Away from the Water Shirley* by John Burningham (Red Fox, 1992).

Resources

Beach hut backdrop, sand tray, pebbles and shells, deckchairs, bunting, books to read on a sun-lounger, towel, buckets and spades, fishing nets, ice-cream stand, washed up boat wreckage, LEGO boats, metal detector for treasure hunting, life jackets, message in a bottle/balloon tag, plastic fish/sea animals, crazy golf, lifeboat, flags and warning signs, crabbing nets

Characters

Families

Café staff or ice-cream seller

Fishermen

Lifeguard

Lifeboat crew

Dog

Predicaments

Discover a message in a bottle or balloon tag

Find a treasure map with directions to lost treasure

A mermaid appears

Shark fin seen

Teacher in role

Lifeguard rescue in a lifeboat

Find a treasure map washed up on the beach

Ice cream seller who is unwell and can't work

Owner of a lost dog

A fisherman who needs help repairing his boat

Texts
Sunk by Rob Biddulph

(HarperCollins, 2017)

The Little Boat by Kathy Henderson

(Walker, 1997)

The Mousehole Cat by Antonia Barber

(Walker Books Ltd, 1993)

At the Beach by Roland Harvey

(Allen & Unwin, 2007)

Writing
Postcard

Message in a bottle

Treasure map

Instructions: how to build a sand castle

Warning signs, e.g. deep water

Boat repair manual

Signs for café/ice cream shop

UNDER THE SEA

Based on *Flotsam* by David Weisner (Clarion, 2012).

Resources
Blue crepe paper/blue cellophane, sand/yellow paper, shells, treasure boxes, pebbles/rocks, diving resources, underwater camera, torch

Characters
King Neptune

Mermaids

Fish, sharks, eels, crabs, lobsters and other sea-life animals

Pirates/divers

Predicaments
Baby fish gets lost

Pirates steal a magic shell/trident belonging to the King

Shark seen near the entrance to the cave

A diver gets stuck in the cave

Teacher in role
Mermaid from another part of the ocean wants to find a new home

A fish is scared of the sharks; how and where can they hide?

A fish who has found a new shipwreck

A deep sea diver wants to interview the sea-life and maybe capture them

King Neptune asking for help to organise an ocean ball for his daughter

Texts
The Rainbow Fish by Marcus Pfeiffer

(North-South Books, 2007)

Mermaid Poems by Claire Bevan

(Pan MacMillan, 2005)

The Fish Who Could Wish by John Bush

(Oxford University Press, 2008)

Little Turtle and the Song of the Sea by Sheridan Cain

(Magi Publications, 2001)

Writing
Treasure maps of the ocean

Messages in the sand made in shells

Menu for 'The Mermaid Ball'

Invitations to a party in the cave

Signs for the cave

Message in a bottle

A WORLD WAR II AIR RAID SHELTER

Resources

Corrugated cardboard, bench, lamp, tins and packets of food, ration books, ID cards, documents, clothes, blackout material, tin mugs, old wireless, old newspaper articles, first aid kit, knitting needles, books, posters, pamphlets, 1940s recipes, gas masks, masking tape on classroom windows, radio, recordings of radio news broadcasts

Characters

Home guard warden

Children/evacuees

People from the community

Land army girls

Soldiers home on leave

Predicaments

Radio announces long night ahead, what will we do to keep busy?

Neighbouring family forced to share shelter as their home is bombed

All arrive safely except one child, bombs overhead – do they go to look for her?

Cooking with limited resources for a birthday

People arrive with little room or food to spare

Teacher in role

Air Raid Warden to inspect safety and food supplies

Doctor asks for help after a raid to set up shelter as medical station

Disoriented stranger lost after an air attack

An injured, hungry German pilot has been shot down and needs help

Mother tells children they will be evacuated in the morning – how will we prepare?

Texts

Archie's War by Marcia Williams

(Walker, 2014)

Goodnight Mr Tom by Michele Magorian

(Penguin, 2014)

Blitzcat by Robert Westall

(Pan MacMillan, 2015)

Rose Blanche by Ian McEwan

(Random House, 2004)

Carrie's War by Nina Bawden

(Penguin, 2014)

Wave Me Goodbye by Jacqueline Wilson

(Random House, 2018)

My Secret War Diary by Flossie Albright

(Walker Books Ltd, 2015)

War Boy by Michael Foreman

(Anover, 2006)

Writing

Letters from an evacuee to parents back home or to an absent father

Papers, letters or maps that have been found

Ration books

News items for a local newspaper

Diary entries of the family or evacuee

Posters to alert people to unexploded bombs or unstable buildings

A VICTORIAN WORKHOUSE

Resources

Tattered cloth, bench, lamp, daily timetable, prayer book, task list (artefacts from the Victorian era including crushing stones, Oakum picking and making flannel), rules for casual paupers, bowl of gruel, bread and cheese, Victorian clothing

Characters
Child
Relieving Officer
Medical Officer
Master/Mistress of the house

Predicaments
A new child is brought into the workhouse
Falling ill in the workhouse
Child is confused over tasks to complete
Planning to escape from the workhouse
Scavenging for extra food

Teacher in role
New child finding out about the rules of the workhouse
Master of the workhouse explaining the daily routine
Officer demonstrating one of the tasks
Relieving Officer interviewing a child
Inspecting the cleanliness of the workhouse

Texts
The Workhouse Girl by Dilly Court

(Arrow, 2013)

Victorian Workhouse (My Story) by Pamela Oldfield

(Scholastic, 2008)

Lady Daisy by Dick King-Smith

(Puffin, 1993)

Street Child by Berlie Doherty

(Collins, 2009)

Workhouse Child by Maggie Hope

(Ebury Press, 2015)

Writing

Writing instructions for one of the tasks

Rules of the workhouse

Letter or diary entry from officer depicting life in the workhouse

Warning signs to display around the workhouse

A spoken monologue by one of the children in the workhouse